GAMES
For all
Occasions

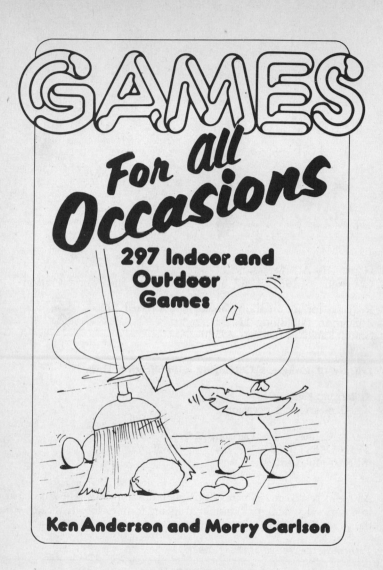

GAMES

For all Occasions

297 Indoor and Outdoor Games

Ken Anderson and Morry Carlson

ZondervanPublishingHouse
Grand Rapids, Michigan

A Division of HarperCollinsPublishers

GAMES FOR ALL OCCASIONS
Copyright © 1951, 1967 by Ken Anderson and Morry Carlson

Requests for information should be addressed to:
Zondervan Publishing House
Grand Rapids, Michigan 49530

Library of Congress Cataloging-in-Publication Data

Anderson, Ken, 1917-
    Games for all occasions.

    1. Games.   I. Carlson, Morry.   II. Title.
GV1201.A58 1988   794   88-55
ISBN 0-310-20151-9

Printed in the United States of America

00 01 02 /DH/ 49 48

CONTENTS

Indoor Games

I. Paper Cutting Race

Take several newspaper sheets and thumbtack each newspaper by the upper lefthand corner to the wall. Then give scissors to each guest and instruct him that he is to cut the newspaper in zigzag fashion so that it will become a long strand, reaching across the room. The first one to make his strand reach across the room is the winner. Anyone who breaks his, automatically disqualifies. Or, if you wish, let anyone who breaks his strand go to a distant room for a piece of mending tape.

2. Feather Race

Give each of your contestants a knife with a feather, leaf or some other light object on it. The idea is to see who can go across the room and back again, keeping the elusive object on his knife. If the object blows off, it must be replaced before the contestant can continue.

3. Roll the Peanut

Give each volunteer a peanut, which he must roll by the nose or chin, or the top of his head if he wants to, across the floor of the living room. Hard boiled eggs, potatoes and similar objects can also be used. If a larger object is used, you might specify that the object cannot be pushed ahead but must be kept in contact with the contestant's nose throughout the race.

4. Air Race

Stretch several strings across the living room, making sure that each of them is tight and will not come loose. Make several small, light airplanes, one for each string, and hang each by its nose or tail by means of a hole threaded through the string. The hole should be the size of a paper punch, so that the airplane will move easily along the race course.

Line up your contestants and at the signal "Go," each proceeds to blow his airplane across the string to see who can reach the goal line first. Anyone who in any way touches his airplane or the string is automatically disqualified.

This can be played with co-pilots, each alternately blowing the plane. If co-pilots are used, let the plane be blown across the string and back again to the initial starting point.

Use any bits of local color, such as pilot's gear, to add to the merriment.

5. Turtle Race

Using heavy cardboard, cut out a number of turtles about twelve inches long and proportionate in width. Cut a small hole through the back of each turtle, about one-fourth of the distance from the turtle's head and about three-fourths of the distance from the turtle's tail, and exactly in the center at that portion of the turtle. Thread a string about thirty feet long through this hole.

Each team in the turtle race must have two members. Start all the turtles at one end, at the beginning of each string. At the opposite end of the string the other contestant must hold the string down to the floor with his toe. Then, by jiggling the string sideways and up and down, whichever proves more successful, each contestant endeavors to make his turtle hop along the length of the string until its head touches the toe of the contestant at the other end. However, at no time should any turtle leave the floor. He may stand upright, but he may not leave the floor. Thus, as the turtle moves along toward his goal, the one who is manipulating the string will be lifting his arm higher and higher.

If you wish you may have the turtle go across the string, and then be returned again to the one who first manipulated the turtle's movements. He must then place the string underneath the toe of his foot, and keep it there securely.

This race will be more successful if the race course is not a carpeted area.

6. Parlor Archery

A needle, with a short piece of thread attached to it, makes an excellent throwing dart. Beforehand, test a half dozen needles getting the right size thread in each. Then put some kind of a cloth target on the wall, and let your guests in turn try their skill.

If played by teams, use colored thread to identify the throws and points earned of each team.

7. Parlor Basketball

At each end of the room have someone standing on a chair. Each one holds out his arms in the shape of a basketball goal. Select two sides, with not more than four on a side. Three would be better.

Using an oval-shaped toy balloon as a basketball, and making sure you have a referee who knows the basic rules of the game, set the fun in motion.

Baskets can be used, if it is convenient to fix them in place. Backstops can be of cloth, since cloth will be strong enough to withstand any pressure from the balloon.

8. Soccer

Using the living room carpet as your playing field, and a balloon as the soccer ball, you can stage a soccer game throbbing with excitement. Limit your teams to four or five on a side, letting the remainder of the guests serve as the cheering section. Arm each contestant with a fan. The ball is moved across the field in either direction by fanning. Its progress can be retarded by the opposing team only with the use of a fan.

If anyone touches the ball in any way, either with his person or with the fan, his team is penalized half way to the goal line. Each time one team is able to fan the ball across the opposing goal line, that team chalks up a point.

9. Parlor Football

Use a large table, preferably a ping-pong table. Allow six or eight contestants on each team. Two contestants defend the goal. Two remain in the back court. The other two are up near the goal line over which they are trying to send the football. Use a ping-pong ball or a hollow egg. The object is to see who can blow the ball across the opposing goal line. The opposition must try to blow the ball back.

The rules are simple. When a player is blowing his chin must rest on the table. Failure to do so results in a two point safety for the other side. Each touchdown counts six points.

Points after touchdown can be attempted by placing the ball on the one-inch line, with the referee giving the signal to blow. If this is done, great care must be exerted to detect offside infractions.

10. Kick for Coffin Corner

Have each of your guests try kicking one of his shoes toward a designated corner of the room. The one who gets the closest to the corner is the winner. If one shoe stands up in the corner it is to be considered closer than the shoe which is lying down in the corner. If there is a tie, let those who deadlocked kick off the tie.

11. Lemon Golf

Use a lemon for the golf ball and either a broom or a mop for the club. A contestant uses the stick end of the broom or mop, holding the large end up. The idea is to hit the lemon, as one would hit a golf ball, down the fairway, which is across the living room floor. The hole is either a chalk circle about twelve inches in diameter or a string placed in the form of a circle. Or to make it even more difficult, turn a dinner plate upside down, instructing the contestants that the lemon must roll up onto the dinner plate and remain in the small ring there. The one who accomplishes the feat with the least number of strokes is the golf champ of the evening.

Or you can lay out a six hole course, with a few obstacles, and stage a tournament. If you do this it would be wise to have other activity for those not competing.

12. Indoor Baseball

This game is hardly suitable for the average living room, but can be played in basements, recreation rooms and the like. Choose two teams, the same as you would for a sand lot baseball game. In order to play the game properly you must have at least four on each side. Six would be a comfortable maximum, though you might use more.

The team which is in the field has a pitcher, a catcher and a man on each of the bases. A shortstop and outfielders may be used, though they are not necessary.

No one runs in this game, except to field a ball. That is, if the man at bat hits successfully, he still does not run. Instead, the team at bat also has a man on first, a man on second and a man on third. The function of these offensive players will be seen in just a moment.

To play the game successfully you will need a number of various colored balloons. To further simplify the game these balloons should be numbered. Balloons as nearly perfectly round as possible are preferable.

A batter steps up to the plate. The pitcher throws a balloon, which the batter attemps to hit. If he hits a fly, and the fly is caught, and flies will usually be caught, he is out. If he fails to hit the balloon in making a strike, he is out. No three strikes in this game—one strike, you're out. However, fouls give the batter another chance.

The bat is the palm of the player's hand, no fists are allowed. If the batter hits the balloon, and it is not caught, he then takes his numbered balloon and throws it to his teammate who stands at first base. If the numbered balloon gets to first base before one of the defensive players can throw the batted balloon to first base, the runner is safe. If the balloon is hit far enough, the offensive man at first base will attempt to throw it to second base, thus making a two-bagger. Anything beyond a two-base hit is unlikely, although three-base hits and home runs are permissible.

When a runner is on first base, that is, when his balloon is on first base, the next batter comes to the plate. The balloon is pitched and if he hits it successfully the offensive man who holds the first ball on first base must attempt to throw it successfully to second base. As he does, the batter throws the second numbered ball to the runner at first base. The defensive team will try to throw the batted ball to second, to catch the runner there. Or if there is not time to do that, they will attempt to catch the runner out at first base. They might even attempt a double play.

Thus the game continues. Bunting is permitted, and will, in fact, play a significant strategy. Even the catcher or the pitcher can field bunts.

Running with the ball, either after it has been fielded or with the numbered ball which represents the runner, is strictly forbidden. However, if the ball is thrown and falls short of its mark, the one who throws it can run up to where it lands, pick it up and throw it again.

You will need an umpire, most certainly, and if the game

should turn into a rout, which is not likely, a scorekeeper.

Incidentally, this same game can be played to great advantage out-of-doors if you have a supply of five basketballs, volleyballs or beach balls. One of them will be needed to use as the pitched ball, the other four to represent runners as they come to bat.

Your offensive players rotate about the field. That is, after one batter has been at the plate, whether he is out or hits safely, the man who is standing on first base moves to second. The man who is on third comes home and either sits in the batters' box awaiting his turn, or steps to the plate if you have a limited number of players. Everyone bats in turn.

The man who has just batted, then, goes to first base, and waits to catch the numbered ball of the next one who takes his turn at the plate.

13. Soap Bubble Race

About three teams, with three on a team, are sufficient for this game. One team member in each group is given a soap-bubble blower with an ample supply of soapy water. The other two members of each team are given fans.

At the signal "Go," each soap blower from each team blows a bubble. The other two team members then proceed to try to fan that bubble across the room. The soap blower follows behind them. If any team's soap bubble breaks before it can be fanned across the goal line, then the soap bubble blower blows another bubble at the point where the last one broke. The first team to get a soap bubble across the goal line is the victor.

Use a committee of judges to see to it that everything proceeds according to Hoyle.

14. Eskimo Relay

This is good for lots of laughs and an equal supply of excitement. You may use two teams or more, but it is best to have five or six on each team.

13

Place each team in line with the players standing behind each other about three feet apart. Give the first one in each line a large ice cube. At the signal "Go," each leader turns and places the ice cube on the neck of the one behind him, who must stoop over. That one tries to balance the ice cube as long as he can. As soon as it slips he must either catch it or pick it up from the floor, then turn immediately and place it on the neck of the next person. This continues until the ice cube has gone all the way to the end of the line, and has been placed on the neck of the one who started the procedure, who slipped to the back as soon as the race started. All of the others remain in their positions.

The winning team is not the one which gets the ice cube to the end of the line first, but the one which is able to take the longest time to get the ice cube to the end of the line! Have a committee of judges on hand to see to it that no one dawdles along the way. As soon as an ice cube is dropped, it must be immediately picked up and placed on the neck of the next person. The only delay of time can come about when one is able to keep the ice cube from slipping off his neck.

The use of hands is strictly forbidden except in moving the ice cube from one person to another. Make the ice cubes of sufficient size so that there will be no danger of their melting before they cover their course.

A variation of this game is to place the ice cube on the top of the hand, with each contestant holding it there as long as possible. Individuals or teams can compete.

15. Necktie Relay

Divide your male guests into two or more teams. Instruct each contestant to take off his coat, vest and necktie. The first member of each team is given a cheap or battered necktie and at the signal "Go," must put on the necktie, then take it off and hand it to the next one in line. This continues until each contestant has put on the necktie, removed it and passed it on down the line. The first team through is the winner.

Assign an impartial judge to make sure that each contestant properly dons his tie before removing it. Do not insist on anything fancy, just be sure the tie is correctly knotted and drawn into place.

16. Ice Cube Relays

Divide your guests into two groups. Each of these teams in turn breaks up into two groups, one at one end of the room, the other at the opposite end. Give each of these four groups a knife. Place two ice cubes on a tray.

At the signal "Go," the first two contestants must each try to slide an ice cube onto his knife, carry it across the room and place it on the knife of the next contestant, who then carries it back and gives it to the one waiting at the other side. This continues until one of the sides has passed the ice cube from contestant to contestant and becomes the first one to successfully carry out the relay. If an ice cube drops, the player is not disqualified, but must stoop down and scoop it back on his knife without using his other hand.

17. Peas on the Knife

Place two bowls of peas at one end of the room and two empty bowls at the opposite end. Have an equal amount of peas in each bowl. Select two teams and give the first one in each line a knife. They run to the bowl and scoop up as many peas on the knife as they can, bring them back and dump them into the empty bowl at the point from which they started. They then give the knives to the next contestants in line, who repeat the procedure.

The team which first transfers its peas from the one bowl to the other is the winner. Any peas which fall along the way must also be picked up on the knife and brought to the bowl. These peas can be left until the very last, if desired. All peas must be retrieved, though, before a victor can be named.

Because of the nature of this relay some team members may

15

have more than one turn. Keep a sharp eye open so that experts aren't pushed ahead of blunderers the second time around.

18. Spoon and Bean Relay

Divide your guests into two or more teams. Half of each team stands at one end of the room, the other half at the other. Each team member is given a spoon which he holds in his mouth. The first contestant of each team places two beans in his spoon and at the signal "Go," hurries across the room to the waiting contestant at the other goal.

Holding his hands behind his back, the contestant with the beans must put the beans from his spoon into the spoon of the other. If a bean drops he must pick it up and put it back into his spoon, and attempt again to put it into the spoon of the other. As soon as the two beans have been put into the other spoon, that contestant hurries back across to the other side and does the same. If a bean drops out of the spoon while a player is going from one goal to the other he must stop and replace it.

Instead of a relay, contestants on each team can also stand in a line and pass the beans from spoon to spoon.

19. A Foot at a Time

This is a race in which each contestant must put one foot directly in front of the other as he goes from the starting line to the goal line. At no time must there be any space between his feet. Sound the warning at the outset that rule infraction will result in disqualification.

20. Shoes in the Target

Divide your guests into two or more teams. Place a basket or large box a distance of ten or fifteen feet from the starting point. Each contestant of each team is given a chance to kick each of his shoes into the basket. At the close of the game count up the shoes and see which team netted the most points.

21. Changed Attire

Divide your guests into two groups. One group leaves for another room. Before leaving its members are instructed to carefully study the clothing of the group which is to remain.

While the first group is gone the remaining group has two of its members change some item of attire. Two of the men may change neckties. Two of the girls may change shoes. The first group then returns and tries to discover who has done the changing.

Next time reverse the order.

22. Find the Clock

Use an alarm clock which ticks at a normal volume. While all of your guests turn their backs or hide their eyes, the alarm clock is hidden somewhere in the room. Then while music is played softly, so as to kill the sound of the clock, the guests move about the room trying to discover where the clock is hidden. As soon as each guest thinks he knows where the clock is hidden he comes to the leader and whispers in his ear. If he has the location correct he may sit down.

23. Bulls-eye

Place a chair in the middle of the room. Set an empty milk bottle directly behind the chair. Use six clothespins, more if you like. Each contestant has his turn. Resting on his knees on the chair, and leaning over the back of the chair, he must try to drop each of the clothespins through the lid of the empty milk bottle. A hard and fast rule is that no one may lower his hand farther than the top of the chair.

24. Bean Race

Have your contestants stand or sit around a table, in the center of which is a bowl full of dried navy beans. Each contestant has a beverage straw and at the signal "Go," each tries to see how many of the beans he can take out of the bowl and place in a cup before him. The object is to suck the beans up with the straw and hold the bean in place by putting the tip of the tongue on the end of the straw. Any bean dropped between the bowl and the cup is disqualified.

25. Cotton Throw

For a bit of variation at your indoor party bring out a ball of soft, fluffy cotton. Make a mark, and see who can throw the ball of cotton the farthest. If your living room is of any size at all, you probably will not have anyone who can throw the cotton across the room.

26. Soup Race

Not more than four can play this game at one time. Get four bowls and, ahead of time, place some vegetable coloring paste around the top of each bowl. Only a little bit is necessary.

Then carefully fill each bowl with water up to within about a half inch of the ring of vegetable coloring just above the water line. Stand each contestant in the center of the room. At the signal "Go," each rushes and picks up a bowl. He must carry the bowl across the room, touch the opposite wall, return and place it on the table. Speed is not the object here, but rather steadiness of hand, because if any contestant allows the water to lap up onto the coloring, so that the water is no longer completely clear, he is disqualified.

27. Powers of Observation

Let your guests make a thorough survey of the living room. Then send them all into another room while you make a number of alterations in the living room. Be sure to write these alterations down yourself, so as not to make any mistake. Call your guests back and give each a pencil and paper with instructions to write down all the changes noticeable. The guest with the largest number of correct answers wins.

Typical changes might be: 1. Switch lamp shades. 2. Move a lamp from one part of room to other. 3. Move a large chair to another position. 4. Change pictures. 5. Switch a dim light bulb with a bright light bulb. 6. Move a throw rug. 7. Draw or lift a window shade.

28. Paper Sculpturing

Give each guest a sheet of newspaper with instructions that each one is to tear out the profile of some person or place familiar to everyone in the group. Then turn out the lights for about five minutes while everyone goes to work.

Or, if you want only half of your guests to be engaged in this game, have those competing hold the newspaper sheets behind their backs as they tear. This will provide a lot of laughter for the other guests.

29. Hit the Dummy

Someone who is *It* stands with his back to the group. Then a bean bag, pillow or some similar soft object is passed about the group, and someone is designated from the group to throw the object at the dummy. As soon as the dummy is hit he turns around and tries to guess, by examining the expressions on the faces of those before him, who it was who hit him. If he guesses correctly that person becomes the dummy. If not, *It* must be the dummy another time.

30. Horses Don't Fly

Your guests stand in a circle, with someone who is *It* in the center. *It* moves his arms up and down as a bird and says, "This is the way birds fly." All of the other guests must

19

do what he is doing. After a bit he changes and says, "This is the way horses gallop." Then the other guests must stop the flying motion and begin galloping, except that It in the center continues to move his arms in a flying motion. To further confuse the contestants, It may change from the motion of a bird to some other creature. If he ever catches anyone not doing the proper motion, however, that one goes into the circle and becomes It.

31. Parlor Hide and Seek

One of your guests is blindfolded and sent out of the room. The remaining guests hide themselves in various places about the room. Then the blindfolded guest returns, and tries to find those who are hidden. Once found, the guest must reveal his identity, and the first one found is It for the next round.

32. Vocabulary Experts

Seat your guests in a circle. Someone within the circle is It. It points to someone, and calls any letter of the alphabet, with perhaps the exception of X· Then while he counts to ten the person to whom he has pointed must give a proper name starting with that letter. Limit it to Bible names, if you wish. If he fails to give a name within the counting time he must give up his place to It.

33. Basket of Fruit

Have your guests sit in a circle with someone in the center of the circle who is It. Have your guests number off by fours. Instruct the *ones* that they are lemons, the *twos* are oranges, the *threes* are apples and the *fours* are bananas.

It will then call off one of these four fruits. When he does every one who belongs to that class must change places with some other from the same group. The three remaining fruits keep their places. While the change is going about It tries to steal one of the seats. If he does the one left without a place to sit down becomes *It* and the one who was *It* becomes one of that kind of fruit.

Occasionally the one who is *It* can shout, "Fruit basket upset!" When he does this, everyone must find a different seat.

34. Earth! Water! Air! Fire!

Divide your guests into two groups and have each group seated in a long line facing the other group. Take a handkerchief and knot it at one end so that it can be easily thrown back and forth between the two groups. Give the handkerchief to someone in one of the groups, instructing him to throw it into the lap of someone in the opposite line. As he throws it he is to call out either "Earth!" "Water!" "Air!" or "Fire!"

If he calls out "Earth" or "Water" or "Air," the one into whose lap he throws the handkerchief must name some bird or animal which lives or moves about in that environment. For example, if he shouts "Earth!" the one into whose lap the handkerchief falls might answer, "Worms!" It would be just as correct, however, for him to name any beast which moves upon the earth.

However, if the handkerchief is thrown, and the one who throws it calls out, "Fire!" then the one into whose lap it falls must remain perfectly silent. If he does not he is out of the game.

As soon as the handkerchief lands in someone's lap the one who threw it begins to count rapidly to ten. If an answer is not given, that is, if either of the three words except "fire" has been called out, then that one is disqualified from the game. This continues until all the members of one of the sides have been disqualified.

35. Electric Current

All of your guests stand in a circle, holding hands. Have someone volunteer to be *It* and stand in the center. While *It* closes his eyes for a moment someone is designated to begin the electric current going about the circle. The current travels by someone squeezing someone else's hand. The electric current does not appear in more than one place at a time, and moves along continuously. That is, it cannot jump from one hand beyond two or three other people. It must go from hand to hand.

The object of those in the circle is to keep the electricity moving around the circle without It being able to point to where the current is. If he does discover that, by quickly seeing someone squeeze another person's hand, then that one goes in the center, and It returns to the circle.

The current comes to a standstill when It looks directly at the one who has last received the electricity.

36. Ring on the String

Get a long string, tied so as to form a continuous circle. Have the string just large enough so that with your guests sitting in a circle each one can hold onto it.

Then place a ring on the string, with the idea that the guests, who always keep their hands clasped to the string, must move the ring from hand to hand and from guest to guest without It who stands in the center, knowing who has the ring. As soon as It discovers who has the ring, that one goes into the center, and It takes his place.

37. Where's the Coin?

Seat your guests around a table, preferably a round table. Choose someone to be It. The other guests sit with their hands underneath the table and pass a coin, a quarter is most suitable, between them. At any time It may call, "Hands up!" At that signal each contestant brings up his hands, with his fists closed, and rests his elbows on the table. Then when It calls, "Hands down!" everyone quickly puts his hands down onto the table in unison. It must then try to discern which one of the contestants had the coin in his hand and slapped it down on the table as the hands went down. If he fails to guess the hands go underneath the table, and the coin is again passed around. However, if *It* succeeds in guessing who has the coin, then that person becomes *It*.

If your group is large you may use more than one coin.

38. Dodge the Pendulum

This game needs to be played in a gymnasium or recreation room. Contestants stand in a circle with the one who is *It* in the center. *It* holds a cord, equal in length to the radius of the circle. On the end of the cord is an old shoe, rubber or the like.

It slowly begins swinging the pendulum around, letting the cord out bit by bit until the object on the end reaches the contestants. Then the contestants must jump over the object as it comes underneath them. If the object hits any of them that one is automatically out. This continues until every one has been put out.

39. Hot Potato

Your guests sit in a circle and someone who is *It* stays on his knees in the middle of the circle. A potato is used, which must be thrown from guest to guest. It is a hot potato and if anyone holds it while *It* counts to ten he is automatically *It*." However, if anyone drops the potato, and *It* gets it, that one is in the circle. Or if anyone throws the potato, and *It* intercepts it, then the one who threw it must go into the center, and *It* returns to the circle.

40. This is My Ear

Have your guests stand in a circle, with the exception of *It* who stands in the center. *It* points to anyone in the circle,

23

and, for example, touches his ear. However, he does not say, "This is my ear," but says for example, "This is my elbow." The one to whom he has pointed must then point to his elbow and say, "This is my ear," while *It* counts to ten. If he fails to do so he becomes *It*. If he succeeds, *It* must go to someone else.

41. Rhymes

Your guests stand or sit in a circle, with someone who is *It* in the center. *It* may turn and point to anyone in the circle and call out some simple word. When he does the one to whom he points must give a word rhyming with that word before *It* counts to ten. If he fails to, or if he gives a word which does not rhyme or has been used before, he goes into the center and becomes *It*. For example, if *It* were to call out the word, "Money," then the one to whom he points might answer with the word "Funny."

42. Bible Vocabulary

Arrange your guests in a circle. Someone who is *It* stands in the center. He goes to any member of the circle, points to that person and says either city, country, man or maid. Then he proceeds to count rapidly to ten. While he is counting, the one to whom he is pointing must answer with some person or place in the Bible.

For example, suppose *It* shouts, "City!" The one to whom he points might answer, "Jerusalem." If he were to say, "Man," then the one in the circle would say, "Abraham."

However, if the one to whom *It* points is unable to give a correct reply, before *It* counts to ten, then he must go into the circle and *It* takes his place.

43. Sense of Touch

Each contestant is given a sack and each sack contains an equal number of objects. Objects used might be such things

24

as a ball, a spool, a stick of gum and other not easily defined objects.

As the leader calls out some object each guest must thrust his hand into his sack and before the leader has counted to ten bring out the object called for. If he succeeds in bringing out the correct object he places it to one side. If he does not succeed that object remains in the sack. The point is to see who can bring out the most correct objects during the calling off of the various items each sack contains.

44. Builders

Have someone draw a church. However, draw it in such fashion that it can be cut into a number of understandable parts. Then give each guest a part of the church, together with a thumb tack. Also, have your guests count off in numbers and try to have the parts mixed up so that the numbers will not tend toward a logical order for assembling the church. As each person's number is called he goes to the wall and puts up his piece where he thinks it ought to be in the over-all structure of the church.

The result may make a rather odd looking sight. On the other hand it might be quite unique.

45. Jumbled Alphabet

Give each of your guests a large supply of alphabet macaroni, and then a simple Scripture verse which each one is to spell out, using only the letters found in the macaroni. See who can spell out the verse first.

Or, if you want a little bit more excitement, dump all the macaroni in the center of the table and let the guests dig into that source.

*   *   *

46. Bible Vocabulary

Seat your guests in a line or semicircle. As they sit, they are to keep time in unison by hitting first their knees, then lightly clapping their hands, then spreading their hands (snapping fingers as they do) before bringing them back in rhythm to hit their knees again. In other words, they are keeping time to the count of three.

Let the one at the foot of the line begin, as he is the one who is going to try to work his way up to the head of the line. Each guest must remember his number, and the guest's number will change as he moves around either up toward the front or toward the back of the line. Begin with the word Bible. That means that the next person whose number is called must give a proper name or place from the Bible, beginning with the letter E, since E is the last letter in the word Bible. Suppose the person at the back of his line calls out, "Number twelve." The person who is twelfth from the head must then give a word such as "Enoch." After he has given the word "Enoch," which he must give before the rhythm has gone through from the hitting of the knees to the clapping of the hands and the snapping of the fingers, then he must wait and call some other number when the time for snapping of fingers comes. Supposing he calls, "Number eight." Number eight must then give a word beginning with H, since H is the last letter in "Enoch."

Suppose that number eight fails to give a word. He then goes to the foot of the line and everyone else from eight downward advances one number. The one who called out, when eight went to the foot of the line, then has a chance to call out and try to get someone else to go to the foot of the line.

Keep in mind that no word should be given except on the snap of the fingers, which is the third motion in the rhythm of which all take part. Also, no number is to be called except at the snap of the fingers. Anyone who gives a word before or after the snap of the fingers automatically goes to the foot of the line.

*   *   *

26

47. Bible Occupations

Divide your guests into two groups. Each group must have an even number of contestants. Pass out to each group identical slips of paper. On half of the slips of paper passed out to each group is the name of a Bible character, on the other half, the name of an occupation. At the signal "Go," the contestants on each team must try to find their matches. The first group through with the correct match wins.

If you wish you may have a referee for each group, who has the correct matches on a concealed sheet of paper. He can be consulted by anyone who thinks he has found his match, but may give information only in the affirmative or negative when asked whether or not the match is correct. This could also be used as an introductory game when you wish to pair up partners for the evening.

Characters and occupations which you might use are: Nimrod, hunter; Noah, ship builder; Matthew, tax collector; Peter, fisherman; Luke—physician; New Testament Joseph, carpenter; Pilate, governor; Lydia, seller of purple; Nebuchadnezzar, Babylonian king; Uzziah, king of Judah; Old Testament Joseph, prime minister of Egypt.

48. Double Meaning

Send one of your guests into another room. While he is gone have the remaining group select some word which has a double meaning. Take the word "train," as an example. The idea is that, when the one who has been sent out returns, those who remain will carry on a lengthy conversation. However, whenever the word "train" would appear in the conversation, the word "blank" would be substituted.

For example: "I like to ride on a blank." "He is going to blank to be a champion."

This continues until the one who is sent out is able to guess the left out word. The one who has just given a sentence, when the word is guessed, is the next to leave the group.

Using words with several meanings, such as the words dear, deer, makes it even more confusing.

49. Avoid M

Choose an unwanted letter, M for example. Your guests sit in one line or in a semicircle. Begin at the bottom of the rung. That guest has the privilege of calling the name of anyone in the group. He will probably call the one at the head of the line or near the head of the line as he will want to get to the front as quickly as he can.

The idea is that he is to ask a question which would most logically be answered using the letter M. However, the person whom he asks must not use that letter.

For example, suppose the question is, "What day follows Sunday?" Obviously, the answer is Monday. Nevertheless, in order to keep from going to the end of the line, the one who answers would have to say, "The day before Tuesday," or give some similar answer.

To further confuse the issue have three or four letters as taboo. The answer must be given while the one who asks the question counts to ten at a reasonable pace.

The ones asking questions may use the disliked letter or letters.

50. Omit the E

Statisticians claim that the letter E is used more frequently than any other letter in the alphabet. Inform your guests, whom you have standing in line, of this fact. Then proceed to ask a series of questions, each question asked once of each guest. The question may have the letter E in it but each answer must avoid using the letter E. Allow about twenty seconds for each answer. Any one who uses a word with the letter E in it is automatically out of the running, as is anyone who is unable to give an answer within the allotted time. The answers must be in the form of a sentence, not merely a one word statement.

Questions you might use are such as, "How are you today?" If the contestant answered, "I am fine," he would be automatically out, since fine uses the letter E. However, an answer such as "I am all right," would be suitable.

Ask questions which are of interest to your local group.

51. Relay Spell Down

Divide your guests into two groups, the boys against the girls if you like, and have an old-fashioned spell down. Don't make the words too difficult, because this is going to be a little bit different than the ordinary spell down. Instead of one person spelling the word given, each person can spell only one letter.

Suppose that you begin by giving the word "Propitiate" to one team. The first one in line will give the letter p, the second the letter r, the third the letter o, and so on down the line. However, if anyone gives an incorrect letter that scores a point for the other side.

Always remember who gave the last letter of a word, or who gave the incorrect letter, as the one next to him will begin spelling the next word when that side's turn comes again.

52. Backward Spell Down

Choose a number of rather well known words, limiting them to perhaps not more than six or eight letters in each word. Then have a spell down, except that each contestant, when given a word, must spell it backward. Suppose, for example, you gave the word "Trouble." The contestant would have to spell it e-l-b-u-o-r-t.

For a good laugh at the end, award a prize to the winner, naming him or her the most backward guest at your party.

*   *   *

Musical Games

53. Guess Who's Humming

Place your guests in a circle. Someone who is *It* stands blindfolded in the center. Your guests move slowly around *It* singing a hymn or some other suitable song. *It* cries, "Stop," and the circle comes to a halt, but the guests continue singing. *It* points to one of the guests and all the others immediately stop singing. This person to whom *It* has pointed must continue to hum the melody.

It attempts to guess the name of the one who is humming. If he is successful they exchange places, otherwise the procedure is repeated.

54. Musical Chairs

Count the number of your guests. Suppose you have twenty-four guests; then you place twenty-three chairs in a circle. While someone plays the piano or you play a recording, have your guests march around these chairs. As soon as the music stops every guest is to run and find a chair. Someone will not be able to find a chair and he is automatically out of the game.

The music is played again and while the guests march around you remove another chair. This continues until two guests and only one chair are left, and the guest getting that chair is declared a champion.

If anyone sits down before the music stops that one is automatically out of the game and must leave, taking a chair with him.

55. Verse and Chorus

This is another rhythm game where the guests are guided by the pianist. Seat guests in a line or semicircle. The pianist plays some familiar song which has both verse and chorus.

The pianist may at any time switch from the verse to the chorus. The idea is that when the pianist is playing the verse every one moves his hands as though he is playing a piano. When the pianist switches to the chorus every one in unison lifts his hands and pretends to be leading singing.

Number every one. As the guests change about they must assume a new number, as the idea is to see who can get to the front of the line. For example, whoever sits in the fifth chair in the line always has the number five. If he moves to the eighth chair he then becomes number eight.

Begin with the person at the foot of the line as he is the one who will be wanting to get to the front. At any time he may call anyone's number. Immediately everyone then changes from what he has been doing. Suppose the pianist is playing the chorus of the song, so that everyone is leading the chorus. Even though the pianist will continue playing the chorus, at that time everyone changes to hand motions as though they were playing the piano. Everyone changes, that is, except the one whose number is called. If he forgets and changes like the rest of them he then goes to the foot of the line. However, if he remembers to continue leading singing instead of playing the accompaniment, he may keep his place. Then the one at the foot of the line calls out someone else's number.

Whenever anyone fails to do his part correctly he moves to the foot of the line and everyone from his chair down advances one position.

*   *   *

56. Guided by Music

Send someone who volunteers to be *It* out of the room. While he is out decide some action which he is to perform when he returns. For example you may want him to draw down the window shade. Have him come back into the room as everyone begins to sing some round, such as "Three Blind Mice." When he comes close to doing what he is supposed to do, bring up the volume of the singing. When he is far from doing what he is supposed to do, let the volume die down.

When he does what he is supposed to do, bring the volume of the song to its highest peak, and add a generous round of applause.

57. Everybody Sings

Your guests stand in a row while someone sits at the piano. The one at the piano plays short excerpts of well-known hymns. Each guest, in his turn, must sing or recite the lines of either verse of the hymn or chorus, which fits the bars of music being played. Knowing the title of the hymn is not enough. If anyone fails to do so he is out of the game.

58. Musical I. Q.

Choose two sides. As the pianist plays excerpts of hymns the first contestant to name the hymn earns a point for his side. As soon as a contestant has earned five points for his side he sits down.

59. What Time Is It?

Give your contestants a sample of the various times in which hymns are written. Then, after the order of a spell down, have a pianist play hymns and give each contestant, in his turn, a chance to tell what time the music is written in.

60.   Verse or Chorus?

Another spell down can be done around favorite hymns. Have the pianist play excerpts only and the contestant must tell whether the excerpt is part of a verse or of a chorus.

61.   Whistle the Next Line

This is another spell down type of game. The pianist plays one line of a hymn and the contestant must correctly whistle the next line.

62.   Hymn Geography

Select hymns, or portions of hymns, which have something to do with geography, and see how many points each contestant can earn by naming what geographical factor the hymn suggests. For example, "The Old Rugged Cross" suggests a hill and "The Stranger of Galilee" suggests a lake, and so on.

This game will work well at a small party.

*   *   *

Icebreakers

63. Humility Contest

Give each of your guests six ribbons of various colors, or some similar marking, to pin on their lapel. No guest is to say "I" for the remainder of the evening. If one guest catches another guest saying "I," he or she is entitled to take one of that guest's ribbons. The one having the most ribbons at the end of the game receives a prize for his contribution toward the cause of humility.

64. Laugh Experts

Call for volunteers to see who can produce the greatest variety of laughter. Award points to the one whose laugh is the most unusual, the one whose laugh is the loudest and the one who brings out the biggest laugh from the audience. From the group, you might name the night's most laughable person.

65. Pantomime Orchestra

Each of your contestants, with the exception of one who is *It*, is a member of the orchestra. Each one is assigned some different instrument to play and while the orchestra is in progress he must pretend to be playing this particular instrument.

The leader, the one who is *It*, plays a violin. The idea is that at any time, *It* may change from playing a violin to that of some instrument in the orchestra. When he does, the one playing that instrument must immediately change to playing the violin. If he does not do it before the leader counts to ten, then he becomes *It* and the one who was *It* takes his instrument and joins the orchestra.

66. Meshach, Shadrach and Abed-nego

Each contestant is called Shadrach. The one sitting on his right is Meshach. The one sitting on his left is Abed-nego. Someone who is *It* stands in the center.

It points to anyone of those seated about him. Suppose he points to you. The person sitting on your right is Mary Smith. The person sitting on your left is John Jones. *It* calls, "Meshach!" Before *It* can count to ten you must give the name "Mary Smith." If you fail to do so you must stand up and give your place to *It*. If *It* had called out, "Abed-nego," then you would have answered, "John Jones."

Now and then *It* may try to fool contestants by calling out Shadrach. A contestant must then answer with his own name, or give up his place.

67. Who Am I?

As your guests arrive pin a slip of paper to each one's back, making sure the guest does not see what is written on the sheet of paper. Use either names of people who are contemporary, great names in history or Bible characters.

The idea is that as the guests move around each guest goes to someone else, moving from person to person, and begins to discuss some of the things that person did. Each person must then endeavor to guess who he is. As soon as a person is successful in guessing who he is he goes and sits down.

Of course the one who is giving information about the other tries to keep it somewhat vague so that person will not be able to sit down before he does.

35

68. Guess Who

Arrange chairs around the room for your guests. Divide your guests into two groups. One of the groups is blindfolded, the other is left without blindfold. Set the blindfolded persons down first, leaving an empty chair between each. The empty chairs are then occupied by those who are not blindfolded.

Starting at the beginning of the line have each guest who is not blindfolded sing some song in a disguised voice. The blindfolded person beside him must try to guess who is singing. If he succeeds, he may remove his blindfold. If he does not, he must await another turn. At intervals have the guests get up and move about in order to further complicate the dilemma of those who have not been able to name the ones sitting beside them. You might arrange it so that the more bashful guests do the guessing instead of the singing, which will probably prove less embarrassing to them.

69. Sober Faces

Line all of your male guests against the wall. Instruct the girls that they are to try to make the men laugh. Each man who laughs is disqualified, and joins the girls—in turn trying to make the other men yet remaining break into smiles.

Give this a surprise ending by awarding some kind of a booby prize to the one who remains the longest, telling him he has been named the biggest kill-joy at the party!

You might ask for volunteers if you think a guest might be embarrassed by this, especially those guests who are new to the group.

70. Yards of Smiles

After your guests have arrived, or while they are arriving, invite each one to enter your smiling contest. Each one puts on the broadest grin he possibly can. Then your judges

36

examine each contestant's face, deciding where the smile begins and where it ends. Using a measuring tape, since it will have to travel in half-moon shape, each entrant's smile is measured.

Award a prize to the man and girl who have the broadest smiles.

71. Sour Puss

Have your guests sit in a circle. The one who is *It* stands in the center of the circle. He goes to any one of those sitting around in the circle and asks all sorts of stupid questions. The one who is asked a question must answer, sensibly or otherwise.

The point is that he must not smile. The one asking the questions may laugh if he wishes, but the one who answers must not smile. If he does he must go into the center of the circle and become *It*.

72. Profiles

You will need one of your artists for this one. As each guest arrives he is taken into a room and asked to stand between a strong light and a smooth wall. Then the artist outlines his profile with a crayon, outlining only the head.

The artist is careful to write the name of each subject on the back of the drawing. When all guests have arrived the profiles are held up to see who can identify the most.

73. Find the Leader

Have your guests sit in a circle. Someone chosen as *It* closes his eyes while someone in the circle is chosen to be the leader. Then while *It* tries to discover who is the leader, the different ones in the circle go through such motions as clapping hands, snapping fingers, stomping feet and the like, always watching the leader to see what to do, and only doing what the leader first begins.

As soon as the leader is caught he goes in the center and becomes *It*.

74. Meet the Joneses

Send each of your guests, except five or six who are in on the game, into an adjoining room. One at a time the guests come out. Each one is told he is to meet the Joneses.

What you do is to imitate the bewildered guest in everything he does. If he clears his throat, you clear your throat. If he scratches his head, you scratch your head. In short, you do everything that he does. You continue to do this until, in exasperation, he sits down.

As soon as a guest sits down, he has met the Joneses, and you call for someone else.

75. Waxing Poetic

Seat your guests in a circle. Get things under way by having someone ask the person to his right a question. He might ask, for example, "What color is my shoe?"

The person of whom he asks the question must answer. He might say, for example, "It's any color but blue." He then turns to the person to his right and asks a question which must be answered in rhyme. Do this until every person in the circle has thus answered.

76. Poetic Partners

Select several pairs of rhyming words such as: Tillie and Willie, moon and June, dove and love, run and gun, coop and soup. Divide your guests into two groups, even numbers of men and women if possible, and give identical sets of these rhyming words to each group. If possible divide them so that all the men will possess the words which rhyme with those possessed by the women.

Next instruct your guests to write a sentence using the last word given. For example, "Once there was a lovely young lady named Tillie." The one who has the word that rhymes with that might write, "One day along came a young gent named Willie." No guest will know what the other guest is writing. Then have your guests try to find the one who has a word rhyming with his phrase.

As soon as they are all lined up have them read their lines, which will constitute a poem. You decide the order in which you want the words read and have the poets line up accordingly.

77. Buzz

Seat your guests in a circle, and begin counting. However when the number seven or any multiple of seven appears, instead of saying the number, the one whose turn has come is to say, "Buzz." For example, one, two, three, four, five, six, buzz, eight, nine, ten, eleven, twelve, thirteen, buzz, fifteen, sixteen, buzz and so forth.

Try to have the guests count as rapidly as possible and eliminate from the ring all those who make a mistake.

78. Opposites

Divide your guests into two groups and seat them facing each other. Someone who is *It* stands between the two lines. He points at someone and asks a question. Or, if he gives only one word, the answer must be a synonym. However, the person to whom he points does not answer, but the answer must come from the one directly opposite in the other line.

If the one in the other line fails to answer he becomes *It*. If the one who is pointed to gets excited and answers, or speaks at all, he is *It*.

This can be made more exciting by having the one who is *It* count rapidly to ten after he asks the question or gives a word. Before he begins to count, however, he says either A or B. If he says A that means the one to whom he is pointing must answer. However, if he says B, it means that the one directly opposite must answer and that A must keep silent.

79. Shoes On and Off

When your guests arrive have each one stand at a line. Ten or fifteen feet away is a basket or a box. Each guest is told to see if he can kick his shoes into the basket or box. If he succeeds he may wear them. If he succeeds in kicking in only one, then he must leave one of them off during the period you decide. If he misses both tries, then he must go without both shoes.

80. Yours for Keeps

This would be good for your Christmas party.

When all your guests have arrived let them sit in a circle. Then bring out a large package and announce that it ıs to be handed from guest to guest around the circle for as long as music is played. As soon as the music stops the one who is holding the package takes off one of the wrappings.

The idea is that the package has many wrappings, each separately tied. In the middle of the package is a fine box of chocolates. The guest who takes off the last wrapping comes to the box of chocolates, and a note saying,, "This is yours for keeps."

*   *   *

Indoor Stunts

81. Pin the Donkey's Tail

This is a new version of the old game of pinning the tail on the donkey. Hang up a large sheet of paper, or bulletin board of some sort on which is the picture of a donkey without a tail. A tail, normal size for the donkey, is cut out. A pin is placed where the tail should hook onto the donkey's body.

Each person in turn puts the head of the pin in his mouth, letting the tail hang from his mouth. Then, while he is blindfolded and with his hands behind his back, he must try to pin the tail onto the donkey.

82. Apple Bobbing

Here is an old Halloween favorite. Get a large tub three-fourths full of water. Then toss into it a liberal supply of apples, all *without* the stems removed. Contestants keep their hands behind their backs, and endeavor to get one of the apples out with their teeth.

83. Deep-Sea Diver

Add a new touch to the old game of bobbing for apples. Use the usual tub of water, but no apples. In their place put some retrievable object which will not float, in the bottom

of the tub. The contestant is kept blindfolded, and must find
the object with his submerged nose, chin or cheek. He then
brings it to the surface with his teeth.

Keep a time record of each contestant's prowess in order
to select the winner.

84. Pennies from the Deep

Another Halloween version of the apple-bobbing stunt is
to place pennies, washers, nails or buttons in a tub. Blindfold
each contestant and give each contestant a mitten to wear on
the hand used in retrieving.

The idea is to see who can come up with the most objects
during the allotted time.

85. Human Calliope

Select eight vocalists from your group who are reasonably
able to stay on pitch. Stand them in line and give each one
a note of the scale to remember. Tune up your calliope with
the piano and instruct each one in the stunt to remember his
note only.

Rehearse a little bit, using the piano to double check, and
make sure that each one remembers his note. Then have each
of the notes bend over, low enough so that their heads can
serve as keys.

Select a musician from your group who can play by ear
and have him play some simple tune by touching the heads
of the various "Notes."

If you have enough musicians, perhaps this would be well
at the party held for your choir members, you might have as
many as fourteen, beginning with the basses and continuing up
through the sopranos. Then the one who plays the human
calliope can work in a bit of harmony.

*   *   *

86. Symphony Concert

All you need for this one is a dozen combs and some paper. Each member of the symphony orchestra holds a comb to his mouth, with a piece of paper on the opposite side. By humming into the comb the paper is caused to vibrate, giving an orchestral effect. If you have those who can hum different parts you can work out some novel musical renditions.

87. Whistling Choir

Ask for the whistlers in your crowd and organize them into a choir. No doubt a number of them will be able to whistle parts, which will make the result all the more pleasing.

88. Organ Concert

Have about six people make up the organ. What they do is hold their hands out, palms up, fingers spread. The fingers are the organ keys.

Then someone serves as the organist. The more ridiculous his get up, the more hilarious the stunt. An organ recording is played, and as the record is played, this organist proceeds to play the organ, pretending that the music is coming from his great console.

For an added laugh, have each one standing in line hold up one of his toes, which can serve as the bass notes for the organist to play on. Also, you might supply the organist with suitable musician's garb.

89. Build a Pyramid

Give each of your guests two dozen matches. Place a quart milk bottle in the center of the room. In his turn each guest places a match across the open top of the bottle. The stack will grow higher and higher until, as one guest tries to put on his match, many of the matches will tumble down. He must add them to his own, and await his turn to put them back on. If one match drops, the contestant must take it back with him.

The one who places all of his matches first on the bottle is the winner, keeping in mind that there can be ties among those who have had an equal number of turns, and the one who is the last one left with matches earns the booby prize.

90. Matches Versus Wits

Use fifteen matches and place them in three piles. Place seven matches in the first pile, five matches in the second pile, three matches in the third pile. Then offer to take on all comers.

Here are the rules. A contestant, and there can only be two in each game, can pick up as many matches as he wants to out of any of the three piles. He may pick up one match if he wants to, he may pick up all of them if he wants to. However, he cannot pick up from more than one pile at a time.

Give your opponent first choice, if he wants it. The idea is that you are to endeavor to make him pick up the last match. Until he is able to make you pick up the last match you remain champion.

The trick to this is very simple. Let your opponent take the lead, but as soon as possible, try to maneuver him into such a place so that you can make only two piles left on the table, each with an even number of matches in them. From then on the going is simple.

One precaution, however. Don't let him catch you with two in each pile!

91. Put on the Steeple

Draw a picture of a church on a large sheet of paper. From a separate piece of paper cut out a fine steeple. Blindfold each guest and have him try to pin on the steeple in the proper place. This is similar to the game of pinning the tail on the donkey.

To add to the fun you might include not only the steeple, but the chimney and the windows and doors and have a number of blindfolded guests participate.

92. Lofty Art

Give each contestant a paper and pencil and some flat, hard substance, such as a book. Each contestant is to draw a picture, perhaps fitting it into a seasonal effect, by holding the paper on top of his head. The one who draws the best picture is the winner.

93. Your Eyes will Deceive You

Draw a square on a piece of paper. Place a medium sized mirror at a slight angle over this paper. That is, the base of the mirror will touch the table on which the paper lies. The top will lean slightly over the paper.

Then give each contestant, as his turn comes, a pencil. Looking into the mirror, not at the paper, he is to draw horizontal lines from corner to corner in the rectangle you have drawn on the paper. To make doubly sure that a contestant doesn't peek, cover the actual paper with some obstacle which you hold in the way. The contestant must then look into the mirror.

The result will be ridiculous to say the least, because the mirror will tell the contestants to draw in one direction, whereas his hand will impulsively go in another direction.

94. Test Your Equilibrium

Place a footstool in the center of the floor. In his turn, each contestant sits on the footstool. He holds his left leg straight out, toe pointing upward. He rests the heel of his right foot on the toes of his left foot. Then, using his left hand to balance he tries to write his name on a piece of paper beside him. Those who are right-handed have the paper on the right side, those who are left-handed have the paper on the left side.

95. Walk the Plank

Place a plank on two blocks, about six inches from the floor. At the end of the plank place a pan full of water. As each guest comes in for his turn of walking the plank, he is permitted to see the pan of water. Then he is blindfolded and instructed that he must keep his hands behind his back. He is to walk to the end of the plank, then jump over the pan.

The hitch is that, while he is blindfolded, the pan is removed. This will make his efforts to jump over the obstacle all the more ludicrous.

96. Plane Trip

Send those who are to make the plane trip into an adjoining room, allowing only one at a time to come out. As each one comes for his ride he is blindfolded. He is then placed on a table leaf, which is held by two strong men, one at each end.

The one taking the ride is instructed to stand on the table leaf, and support himself by placing his hands on the head or shoulders of each of the pilots.

The plane proceeds to take off, and apparently goes high into the air. Actually what happens is that the pilots lower themselves slowly toward the floor, until they are finally on their knees. The one who is taking the ride will think that the board has gone up high, so that he must reach down to steady himself on the heads of the pilots. When the pilots have brought their heads down as far as they can go, the fearful rider is instructed to jump. If he refuses to jump have someone lightly give him a shove from behind, while someone is on hand to steady him if he stumbles.

He will be surprised when he discovers that he only jumps a few inches to the floor!

97. Imitation

Use two soup dishes. Blacken the bottom of one of them over a candle flame and keep the other clean. Put a little water in each one as a means of fooling your prey.

As each guest comes in tell him he is to try to do exactly the same as you do. First the guest sits down directly in front of you, and is instructed to look you squarely in the eye. Then a soup dish is given to you, and one to the guest. You will have the guest do all sorts of things and then gradually have him take his dirty fingers, which he does not know are dirty, from underneath the dish, and make all sorts of smudge marks on his face.

98. O'Henry's Beauty Parlor

Place your guests in another room where each awaits his beauty parlor appointment. As each guest comes he is carefully blindfolded. Then the "beauticians" go through such procedures as striking matches with which to make eye blacking, opening and closing cold cream jars and the like.

However, instead of marking up the face with the burnt end of the match, use the opposite end. Instead of cold cream, use water. You will be able to simulate other objects, so that each guest will think his face is being made a sorry sight.

Then take off the blindfold, and laugh to your heart's content at the strange spectacle. After that, show your guest the mirror, and watch his face register surprise, when he realizes that you did not do anything to it after all!

99. Watch the Birdie!

Rig up a fake, old-fashioned camera. As each guest comes in to have his picture taken, he is met by two photographers of the old-fashioned kind. One of them stands at the camera, and the other one, with his hands behind his back, greets the subject and asks him to sit down.

Then, while the cameraman gets ready to take the picture his assistant stands behind the subject. Using his hands, he turns the subject's face first to one side and then to the other. Finally the picture is taken, and the photographic plate is taken out.

The photographic plate is a mirror, which reveals to the subject that the assistant had blackening all over his hands which was spotted onto the subject's face during the setting up for the picture.

100. Camouflaged Camera

Make a fake camera out of cardboard, trying to set it up on the order of the old-fashioned cameras used by photographers back in the days of the button hook shoe. However, hide an actual camera within this fake camera.

Fix up lights, humorous backgrounds and the like. Get some of your guests to pose as subjects, telling them that you want them to pose the way that they have seen some of their forebears pose in old family pictures. Use mustaches, old-fashioned clothing and whatever else you can get to make it seem the more ridiculous.

Your guests will think they are merely posing for the fun of it. However, after this stunt has worn itself out, prepare yourself for the biggest laugh of all when you take out the actual camera and show the guests that you really took their pictures after all. Pictures will be on display at your next party, or prints can be sent to any guests desiring them.

You will need to be a bit on the ingenious side with this, so that no one will suspect you actually do have a camera inside.

101. Knock Off the Coin

Place a quarter or fifty cent piece on the table, with about one-third of the coin protruding over the edge of the table. Each of your guests approaches the table holding either the right or the left arm directly above his head. Then, coming very quickly, and not stopping to judge distance, each one is to see if he can bring his forefinger down, keeping his arm straight, and flip the coin off the table. His finger must touch only the coin, not the table.

You'll be surprised how few can judge the distance correctly.

102. Move the Coin

Place a nickel, a penny and a quarter on the table. Place the nickel and the quarter on opposite sides from the penny. Then instruct any of your guests to put the quarter between the nickel and the penny, obeying the following rules. The nickel can be moved, but must not be touched. The penny may be touched, but it cannot be moved. You may touch or move the quarter in any way that you wish.

Here is the solution. Push heavily with one finger upon the penny. With the other hand, snap the quarter hard against the penny. If you snap hard enough, it will cause the nickel to jump out of place, leaving ample space for the quarter to be put between the nickel and the penny.

103. What Do You Hold?

Send eight or ten volunteers, as many as want to go, into another room. Then bring out a number of objects, which have been prepared ahead of time, and one by one have each contestant come out into the living room.

Each contestant is blindfolded and instructed to hold out his hands. Various objects are placed in his hands and left there for just a moment, and he is to try to identify them.

Objects could include such items as: raw liver, ice cube,

boiled egg with shell removed, ball of thread, safety pin and the like.

Instruct each contestant that it is not permissible for any of the objects to be fingered. An object can be shaken lightly on the hand, if the contestant desires, but he may not try to identify it by any other means of feeling.

If you wish, keep a list of the ones who can name the most correctly, and award a prize.

104. In the Bucket

Place a large bucket against the wall. Ask for a volunteer who thinks he has a good eye. Give him a dozen potatoes, and tell him he is to carefully judge the position of the bucket, to see how many potatoes he can throw into it while blindfolded.

When the blindfolded contestant throws his first potato, have someone slip over and make sure that the potato falls into the bucket, even if the bucket has to be moved (very quietly) just a little. After that first hit, however, remove the bucket completely, and have your other guests shout all sorts of words of encouragement to the frustrated contestant who can't understand why he does not hit the mark!

When he gets ready to make his twelfth try, you might slip the pail back again, so that when he takes off his blindfold he will wonder how he could come so close so many times without so much as even hitting the bucket.

105. Cut a Pear but Do Not Touch It

Place a pear on the table, together with a knife, and ask your guests if they can cut it in half without touching it. After everyone is convinced it cannot be done, take the pear and tie a string to its stem. Then hang the pear up as high as you can, so that the pear hangs still like the base of a motionless pendulum.

Now place a knife directly beneath the pear. You will need to do a little rehearsing on this so that you can place the knife accurately. Then cut the string with a scissors, and the pear will fall with quite some force, and the knife will cut it in half.

106. Making Paper Stand on End

Bring out a flat piece of thin paper, about three inches wide and five inches high. Lay the paper flat on the table. Challenge anyone to make the paper stand on end without touching it and without leaning it against anything.

Your guests, unless they know the trick, will naturally insist that it cannot be done. So you proceed to show how it is done. Take a comb out of your pocket. Run it through your hair a number of times, and then hold it down to the edge of the paper. The paper will cling to the comb and you will be able to lift it up and stand it on end.

Caution: This stunt will only work in the winter time, and the colder the weather the better.

107. Cotton Boll Race

Place a number of small balls of cotton, depending on the number of contestants you plan to use, in a large bowl in the center of the table. Blindfold your contestants, and give each one a small bowl and a wooden spoon. Instruct your contestants that there are balls of cotton in the large bowl, and that each one is to see how many of those balls he can get into his own bowl. No one can use his hands or tell in any way whether or not he actually has a ball of cotton on his spoon, because the balls are so light.

108. Handicap Wrestling

Two men or boys sit in the center of the room with their backs to each other. Their hands are tied to their ankles, their knees drawn up tightly against their chests. Then they are instructed to wrestle each other, without turning around. The object is that one must try to push the other one down on the floor, without being pushed down to the floor himself.

109. Blindfolded Couples

Get two or three couples to volunteer. Place them some place in the room, twisting them around and around so as to get them all mixed up in directions. Then instruct them to hold hands throughout the search. They must also keep silent.

If any couple breaks handclasps, that couple is automatically out of the game. The object is for each couple to find a certain object or place in the house which you instruct them to find. Not only will they have a hard time finding the object, but they will have an equally hard time deciding which one's way is the way to go.

110. Spoon Pictures

You and one of your guests must team up on this one, getting your signals straight in advance. Then one of you goes out of the room, while the other holds a spoon in front of one of the guests. The partner returns, examines the spoon, and then names the one whose picture was taken.

The trick is very simple. All you do is to sit as nearly as possible in the same manner as the one whose picture was taken.

That is, if he has his feet crossed, you cross yours. If he is sitting toward one side, you do the same.

111. Shoes and Socks

Ask a number of your men guests to volunteer for this one. Each one removes his shoes and socks, which are then placed at one end of the room. Then each of the contestants is blindfolded, during which time the shoes and socks are mixed around.

At the signal "Go," each one races on his hands and knees to the pile of shoes and socks, and puts on the first pair of socks and shoes he can find. First one who has shoes and socks on, the shoes laced and tied, and crawls back to the beginning line is the winner.

You might award a booby prize to the one who puts on the oddest conglomeration, which is sure to happen if there are different colored shoes and socks in the lot.

Also, you can make the thing even funnier by having your contestants first roll up their trouser legs, so that the results of their search will be all the more evident.

112. Costume Contest

Divide your guests into four groups or more, depending on the number in attendance, and send each to a separate room. Supply each group with a generous amount of newspapers and pins, with instructions to select one of the members as a model on which a paper costume of some sort will be made. Then bring all the groups back together again and select the winning costume.

113. Obstacle Race

Send several of your guests into another room and have them return one at a time. When each returns he will find a number of obstacles in the living room. He is told to examine them carefully, as he will be blindfolded and must endeavor to walk across the room without bumping into any of the obstacles.

While he is being blindfolded the obstacles are carefully, quietly moved aside, so that the blindfolded contestant actually has clear sailing.

It will be a good laugh to see him walk in all sorts of contortions across the room, trying to avoid obstacles which do not exist!

114. Psychological Experiment

Send an even number of your guests who want to take part in this game into a room by themselves. Inform them that they are to pair up, and have one pair ready to come on summons.

The guests remaining compose a sentence. For example, "The red airplane landed in the field."

The first two are then called out and given a folded piece of paper containing this sentence. They are then instructed to go into another room, apart from the one they came from, and one of them is to read this sentence. Under no conditions should the other one read it.

While the two are gone, the remaining guests choose a number of words which are to be given to the contestants when they return.

When the contestants return the spokesman from the group in the living room proceeds to name these various words. Contestants are informed that they are to give the first word which comes to mind after the word is named. For example, you might say "Airport." The contestant who had not read the sentence would probably answer something like "Hangar." However, the other one, not wishing to be caught off guard, would deliberate a moment. After you have tried a half dozen or so different words, it should not be difficult to tell which one read the sentence and which one did not.

Let these two then become members of the group in the living room, and bring in another pair for the unique experiment.

*   *   *

Quiz Games

115. Pilgrims and Indians

Choose up sides. One side is the Pilgrims, the other side the Indians. Select a two or three member committee of your sharpest Biblical wits to act as referees, throwing out any questions which in their opinion are not fair.

First, an Indian shoots an arrow, that is, a Bible question, at a Pilgrim. If the Pilgrim answers it, then he can shoot one back at the Indian. If the Indian answers it, then neither side scores. However, whichever contestant fails to answer the Bible question asked him, is automatically out.

If you want to make the game more interesting, you might try this. Suppose an Indian shoots a question at a Pilgrim and the Pilgrim misses. The Pilgrim is not out unless he shoots a question back at the Indian, and the Indian is able to answer it. If the Indian also misses, then both of them remain in the game, just as they would if both of them had answered correctly.

116. Bible Spell Down

Have an old-fashioned spell down some day, using only names and places from the Bible. You might warn your guests beforehand, so they can brush up on some of the difficult ones.

Perhaps you could pit the men against the women in old-fashioned spelling bee style.

117. Bible Quiz-Down

Have your guests stand in a row, or in two groups, contesting against each other. Alternate between persons and places. The first contestant must name some person in the Bible, the next one some place. If you are dealing with two groups, you might have two persons named for each place. There can be no duplications. Anyone who duplicates is out of the game, as well as anyone who is not able to give a person or place not named before when his turn comes.

118. Which Came First?

An interesting Bible game can be built around the chronology of characters and events in the Scriptures. You can get your material from the Bible itself, or from a good Bible history.

Have your guests stand in line, and as each one has his turn, give him two persons, places or events in the Scriptures. He is to name which one came first.

For example, if you were to say, "Peter or Paul?" the correct answer would be "Peter," since the Apostle Paul did not make his appearance until in the Book of Acts, while Peter came in the Gospels. Or if the question were, "Tower of Babel or Walls of Jericho?" the answer would, of course, be "Tower of Babel."

119. Walking Alphabets

Select two sides, with a predetermined number of contestants on each side. Pin a letter of the alphabet on the front of each contestant. Each side has the same selection and amount of letters.

Each side stands in a huddle so that all contestants face each other. The Bible question, one which can be answered with a word spelled by the letters possessed on each side, is asked. As soon as one of the sides determines the correct answer, or what its members think to be the correct answer, those whose letters spell out the answer quickly go and stand in line. The side which correctly spells out the word first gains the point.

120. Bible Occupations

List a number of well-known Bible occupations and the names of those engaged in them. Then give each guest an occupation and give him a chance to name some Bible character who pursued that occupation. Any guest who fails to give a correct answer is automatically out of the game. Also, no one can use the same character twice for any given occupation, although a character who has more than one occupation may be used more than once.

The one conducting the quiz must be careful not to name an occupation if the names of all those who pursued it have been given.

121. Twenty Questions

Limit the contestants in this game to three or four, who are sent out of the room while the remaining guests choose some reasonable subject or object near at hand or remote. Then the contestants return, and are told whether the item they are to guess is animal, vegetable, mineral or abstract.

Animal includes all members of the animal kingdom, as well as man. Vegetable includes anything that grows in the manner of plant life, or anything that is directly derived from that which grows as plant life. Mineral includes all objects such as earth, water, air, ore and derivatives thereof. Abstract would include famous thoughts, motives and the like.

The guests have twenty opportunities to guess the right answer. They can ask anything they wish, but the only answer must be "Yes" or "No." If the questions are asked intelligently, even the most remote object, if it is a fair selection, can be discovered within the limit of twenty questions.

For example, suppose the person you chose was Noah. You would tell the contestants that the subject was animal. Then one of the contestants would ask, "Is the subject a man?" The answer to this would be "Yes." Then one of the contestants might ask, "Is this person living?" The answer to this would be "No." Sooner or later, the contestants would ask, "Has this character anything to do with the Bible?" Then the question would be asked if this person were in the Old or New Testament. Before long, someone would ask if this character had anything to do with judgment, an unusual ministry or the like.

You will be surprised how often a sharp group of quiz experts can guess, in twenty tries, even a difficult item.

*   *   *

Written Games

122. Scrambled Verses

Take a dozen or so familiar Bible verses and rearrange the words in each. Make sure the verses are familiar, since you will only read each verse, as it is scrambled, twice. The object is to see how many of your contestants can unscramble each verse. No one will be asked to unscramble the verse word for word, but to make it quite apparent that he knows what the correct quotation is.

You may use more difficult Bible quotations if you have a mimeograph available, so that you can supply each of your guests with a copy of the scrambled verses, which must be unscrambled within a given length of time.

123. Name the Book

Select a number of outstanding Bible incidents, no more than one from any book of the Old or the New Testament, and then mention these incidents briefly to your guests. Advise the guests that no book will be used twice. See how many can guess which book contains the incident named.

124. Is It In the Bible?

Using a book like *Bartlett's Quotations,* select a number of quotations which are similar in tone to quotations from the Bible. Then, along with these, select a number of quotations from the Bible itself, a few of them from such sources as the book of Proverbs. Mix these together and read them to your guests. See how many can tell which is a Bible reference and which is a non-Scriptural reference.

This can be worded as a true-false test.

125. Incomplete Bible Verses

Read Scripture portions, leaving out words here and there which must be filled in by your guests. Take most of the quotations from familiar verses, adding perhaps one or two which will be recognized only by those who are closer students of the Bible.

126. Find the Errors

Have someone read a well-known Bible story in which several errors have intentionally been written, such as incorrect names, incorrect places, numbers or the like. As the story is read, your guests are supposed to write down all the errors they detect.

127. Gifts of the Bible

At your Christmas party see which guest can list the most gifts spoken of in the Bible.

128. Bible Books

Hold up a number of different objects, each of which in one way or another illustrates some book of the Bible, and see how many of your guests can guess what each object represents. A telephone book, for example, would represent the Book of Numbers. A pair of field glasses could represent the Book of Revelation. One improvised crown could represent First Kings, while two improvised crowns would represent Second Kings. History books could be used to designate First and Second Chronicles. An hour glass, just freshly overturned, could stand for the Book of Genesis. A mark on a piece of paper could represent the book of Mark. A picture from ancient Rome could be for the Book of Romans. Several people rushing out of a door could represent Exodus. You can perhaps add other items to the list.

129. Vocabulary Test

At your Christmas party instruct your guests to see how many words of four letters or less each one can make using only the letters in *Merry Christmas*. No letter may be used more often than it appears in these two words. Another variation of this is to see how many Bible characters or places can be named which begin with one of the letters in *Merry Christmas*. This also can be done with other seasons of the year.

130. Christmas Vocabulary

Give your guests paper and pencils, with instructions to see how many proper names and places related to Christmas each one can name within a given length of time.

131. Change the Letters

Give each of your contestants a pencil and paper and a list of perhaps a dozen four letter words. Make sure beforehand that each of these words can be rearranged so as to form another word by the changing of only one letter. Instruct your guests to see how many words each one can make, within a given length of time, with these words, changing only one letter at a time. For example, suppose the word is "Dope". Words which could be used would be, nope, hope, dote and the like.

132. Telegrams

Here is a game which can be worked into a seasonal item. Give each guest a piece of paper, at the top of which is to be written a word you assign. Using each letter in order from the word, guests are instructed to write a telegram.

For example, supposing it's your Halloween party, and you assign the word *Halloween*. A typical telegram might be: "How awful lest lurking outside we encounter eerie nothings." Award a prize to the best entry.

133. What's in the Sack?

Hang a dozen or so sacks in a row somewhere in your house, and place a different object in each sack. Objects might be such things as alarm clocks, toothbrushes, fountain pens, flashlights, hairbrushes and the like. Each guest is allowed to feel each sack once. He must then write down on a piece of paper what he thinks is contained in each sack.

134. Memory Test

Select a number of unusual objects, along with commonplace objects, and place them on a tray. Allow your guests a minute or two to look at these objects, then remove the tray and give each guest a pencil and paper and instructions to write down as many as he can remember.

135. Finger Tip Quiz

Each of your contestants is blindfolded, or instructed to keep his eyes tightly closed. Then a series of twelve or fifteen objects, such as a potato, a pocket watch, a fountain pen, a book and the like are passed down the line, giving each contestant a chance to feel the object.

After the objects have been passed they are taken out of sight. Then the guests are allowed to remove their blindfolds, or open their eyes, and each one is given a paper and pencil and instructed to write down as many of the objects as he can remember.

136. Guessing Game

Give each of your guests a pencil and paper. Then display a number of objects, asking a question concerning each, the answer to which you must know in advance and have recorded on a piece of paper for quick grading. The following objects and questions are examples of what you could use: 1. The weight in pounds and ounces of a milk bottle. 2. The number of buttons in a small box. 3. The length in inches of a string. 4. The number of pages in a closed book. 5. The number of yards in a spool of thread. 6. The number of words on a particular page shown briefly to the guests. 7. The height in inches of the room. 8. The circumference in inches of a window in the room. 9. The amount represented in postage stamps on a box which you hold briefly before the guests, giving them an opportunity to see the stamps. 10. The exact amount of a dozen pieces of change which you have on a tray and show briefly to your guests.

137. Roman Numerals

Instruct your guests to number ten, twenty or as many entries as you intend to give. Then give arabic numerals, instructing your guests to transpose these into Roman numerals.

138. States and Capitals

You can always test your guests' knowledge of national affairs by listing twenty or so states, and having your guests write down the capitals for each one. Or, for something a bit different, give the capital cities and have the guests give the state.

139. A Girl Named Kate

Read each of the following questions to your guests and have them write down the word which each question suggests. Inform them in advance that each word will have the word "Kate" in it, though not spelled as the girl's name.

1. What Kate is always repeating herself? (Duplicate)
2. What Kate is always destroying things? (Eradicate)
3. What Kate is always making speeches at ceremonies for the opening of new buildings? (Dedicate)
4. What Kate makes the wheels go round? (Lubricate)
5. What Kate is always full of advice? (Advocate)
6. What Kate has been to college? (Educate)
7. What Kate is always out of breath? (Suffocate)
8. What Kate is always able to get out of difficult situations? (Extricate)
9. What Kate serves as a good guide? (Locate or Indicate)
10. What Kate likes chewing gum? (Masticate)

140. Fast Thinking

Each guest is instructed to write down the first twelve words which come to his mind after you have given him his cue. Set a strict time limit. Use such words as moonlight, farm, happiness, church, ocean and the like. Read the reactions, and you will be surprised at the information you will receive concerning the goings on in the minds of your various guests.

141. The Experts Speak

Give a sheet of paper and a pencil to each guest. Instruct each of the men to write on the subject, "How to successfully bake a cake." Instruct each of the women to write on the subject, "The mechanical operation of a gasoline engine."

If you have a large number of guests turn the results over to a committee of judges, who will select the most humorous entries to be read later on in the program. Ask your guests to try to write sincerely, as that may make the results all the more humorous.

142.   Know Your Merchandise

Select a number of well-known slogans from magazine and newspaper advertisements and read them to your guests, or display them, and have the guests write down which merchandise each slogan represents.

143.   Continued Story

Fold a large piece of paper in the shape of a pleated paper fan. Then pass this paper among your guests. On each fold each guest must write some sentence having to do with taking a trip. Instruct the guests to be as original and as humorous as they can. After the paper has made the rounds the pleats are unfolded and the entire story read to the amusement of all.

*   *   *

Picnic Games

144. Doughnut Jump

Tie a number of doughnuts to the end of a string. Each doughnut is held dangling from its string about ten inches above the mouth of each contestant. The idea is to see which contestant can get the most bites out of his doughnut without jerking it loose from its string. Or see which contestant can first eat his doughnut with a minimum amount of waste falling to the ground.

145. Crackers and Whistles

This is an old favorite. Give each of your contestants a half dozen crackers. At the signal "Go," each contestant stuffs the crackers into his mouth and eats them as fast as he can. The object is to see who can whistle first.

146. Cracker Eating Relay

Select two teams or more. Give each contestant a cracker. At the signal "Go," the first member of each team begins to eat his cracker. He may eat as fast as he wishes. The idea is that the second person in line may not begin to eat his cracker until the first one has been able to whistle. This goes right on down the line, until one of the last members of one of the teams is the first one to whistle, thus bringing his team in as champion.

147. Candy Relay

Give each contestant a candy bar. At the signal "Go," each contestant begins eating. The one who is able to whistle first is the winner.

148. Banana Race

Give each contestant a banana, and at the signal "Go," each contestant must peel and eat his banana while holding one hand behind his back. In other words, he will peel the banana with his teeth, then eat it. The first one through, and able to whistle, is the winner.

149. Ice Cream Licking Contest

Give each contestant a big dipper of ice cream, making sure that each dipper is of uniform size, on a full size plate. Each contestant must hold his hands behind his back. To further add to the merriment, put a spoon of chocolate topping on each dip of ice cream.

At the signal "Go," each contestant goes after his ice cream. A judge watches each one to make sure the rules are not broken. Positively no biting—the tongue alone must be used to lap up the ice cream! The one who gets his plate clean first is the winner.

150. Bubble Gum Contest

Give each of your contestants a large stick of bubble gum and see which one can blow the largest bubble. Appoint a committee of judges to decide the winner. Or, if you want to have a bit more hilarity, have each contestant stand with hands behind his back. The object is to see which one can blow six bubbles first. Since fingers are usually needed to put the gum back into the mouth after a bubble has been blown, this will be good for a lot of laughs.

151.   Picking Potatoes

This is a game for individuals. For each individual, string out a dozen potatoes between him and his basket, which stands at the goal line. Try to lay the potatoes of each contestant in a similar manner. Instruct each contestant that he may pick up whichever potato he wants, but only one at a time. He must take each potato to the basket before returning for another. First one through is the winner.

152.   It Is in the Balloons

Divide your contestants into two teams or more. Each member of each team gets a balloon. Ahead of time write out a series of instructions, giving the same instructions in each set of balloons. At the signal "Go," the contestants begin blowing their balloons. They must blow until the balloon bursts so that they can get the instructions which are on a piece of paper inside the balloon.

The idea is that all the contestants in each team must break their balloons so that they can put their instructions together, then follow them out. Have the instructions guide the teams as to where they must go and what they must do, and the first one through wins.

153.   Balloon Relay

This is a shuttle relay in which you have two or more teams, each with an even number of contestants. Half the contestants stand on one goal line, the other half on the other. Give each team a balloon of uniform size. At the signal "Go," the first contestant in each team begins to run, batting the balloon in the air along with him. He cannot catch the balloon, but must keep tapping it with his hands.

The object is for him to bat the balloon down to his waiting teammate at the other goal, who then takes the balloon and bats it back to the other goal, repeating the procedure.

154. Balloon Burst Relay

Divide your contestants into two or more teams, each with an equal number of contestants. Each contestant is given a balloon. At the signal "Go," the first contestant on each team begins blowing his balloon. As soon as his balloon bursts the next contestant may begin blowing.

This continues until one of the teams has been the first one to burst all of its balloons, and is thereby declared the winner.

A variation of this might be to give each contestant a stick of bubble gum, making sure that each contestant knows how to blow bubble gum, and then have the first contestant put the gum in his mouth, chew it and blow a bubble which bursts. As soon as the bubble has been blown and bursts the second contestant may put his gum into his mouth, chew it and do the same. This continues on down the line.

155. Whistling Contest

Each contestant fills his lungs with air to see who can keep whistling the longest. Have sharp-eyed judges on hand to make sure no one pauses or takes an additional breath of air.

156. Back to Back

Have your contestants choose partners, then have each pair stand back to back. Tie their ankles together and have them hook their arms together. Then line the contestants up and at the signal "Go," let them start maneuvering their way to the goal line.

157. Toe Relay

Divide those contestants who will volunteer for this relay into two or more teams, each having an equal number. Half of each team stands at one goal line, the other half at the other, as this is a shuttle relay. Each contestant removes both shoes and socks, and the first contestant places a pencil between the big toe and second toe of either foot. At the signal "Go," each contestant hops down to the other goal as fast as he can, making sure to keep the pencil between his toes.

If the pencil drops out he must stop and replace it as fast as he can without using his hands. Also, when he reaches the other goal, he must give the pencil to his teammate without either of them touching it with his hands.

When the other teammate has it between his toes, he begins hopping back to the other goal, and the procedure is repeated.

158. Under the Blanket

Divide your contestants into teams. Half of the contestants stand at one goal line, half at the other. In between each goal line, fasten securely to the earth an army blanket or canvas for each team. Leave just enough slack so that contestants can wriggle through on the ground underneath the blankets.

The object is for the teams to compete as shuttle relays. The first contestant runs to the blanket, dives underneath and crawls to the other side, gets up and runs and touches the hand of his waiting teammate, who then does the same, returning to the other goal. This continues until each contestant has had his try, and one of the teams comes out victorious.

159. Stiff-legged Race

Bring on several broomsticks or smaller pieces of timber, as well as an ample supply of heavy twine. Each volunteer has a broomstick tied securely to each of his legs, so that he cannot bend either knee. Line up the contestants at the starting line, and see which one can reach the finish line first.

160. Siamese Twins Race

Divide your contestants into pairs and have each pair joined together by the ankles of one foot, that is, the left ankle of one bound by a cord to the right ankle of the other. The pairs line up at the starting line and race to the goal.

161. Keepaway

This is an old favorite in which two teams try to keep a ball from each other. A volley ball or basket ball is preferred.

162. One-Arm Keepaway

This is the same as the regular game of keepaway, except that each contestant must keep his left arm behind him. The ball must be passed and caught using only the right arm.

163. Keepaway Free for All

Divide your contestants into pairs. Give each couple a ball. Each couple throws its ball back and forth, while at the same time trying to intercept a ball from some other couple. As soon as one couple has its ball intercepted, that couple is out of the game.

Couples must not stall for any great length of time. To prevent this make it a rule that no one can intercept the ball of another couple unless he has just thrown or caught his own ball.

Also, if one couple intercepts the ball from another couple, that couple must give all the balls it has gathered to its conquerors.

164. Call a Number

Your contestants form a circle and number off. Each one is instructed to be sure and remember his number. The one who is *It* stands in the center of the circle with a basketball, volleyball, beach ball or some similar object. He throws the ball high into the air and calls a number. The person whose number is called must catch the ball. If he fails to catch it, then he is *It*. If he does catch it, then *It* must throw the ball again and call another number. While *It* is waiting to call a number, the circle must move slowly.

165. Poison Ball

The contestants stand in a circle. The one who is *It* stands in the center of the circle with a basket ball, beach ball or volleyball in his hand. He slowly turns around, looking innocently at each one in the circle. At times he will fake as though he is going to throw at someone. If the one at whom he fakes forgets himself and jumps he is automatically out. On the other hand, if *It* does throw the ball and hits anyone in the feet, he is automatically out.

The idea is that when *It* throws the ball at someone in the circle that one must try to jump to avoid being struck. If *It* hits anyone above the knees, that one is not out. The ball must be thrown below the knees.

166. Targets

Number your guests into two groups. One group forms a circle. The other group stands within the circle. Using a basketball the guests in the circle are to try to see how many of those inside the circle they can eliminate, by hitting them below the knees with the ball. The procedure is to pass the ball around until someone is caught off guard.

After everyone inside the circle has been eliminated the group changes about. Those who did the throwing go inside and become the targets.

167. Wheelbarrow race

Line up your ambitious boys, or the men, if they are game, in pairs. Each pair is to cover a distance of twenty-five yards to a designated line, and then return. Going, one of the contestants in each pair acts as a wheelbarrow. That is, he walks on his hands while his partner holds onto his legs in wheelbarrow fashion. When they reach the first goal line, they change places, and return to the starting point.

168. Endurance Contest

Another version of the wheelbarrow race is to line all the contestants up together. A pacer, walking ahead, leads the way and sees to it that all stay in line. The object is not to see who can complete any distance first, but to see who can keep going the longest. As soon as any one "wheelbarrow" folds his arms and lets his chest come to the ground, he is automatically out.

169. Lobster Race

Contestants race from the starting line to the goal on their hands and knees. However, everyone must progress either backward or sideways. Anyone who goes forward, even for one step, is disqualified.

170. Blindfold Leapfrog

Add new spice to the old childhood game of leapfrog. Divide your contestants into teams of an equal number and blindfold each contestant. First team through is the winner and you will, of course, keep strict rules insisting that every frog must leap over everyone in front of him, no matter how much fumbling it takes him to find his way if he should get off course.

171. Horseback Wrestling

This is a game primarily for young fellows, who should be divided into teams of two members each. One is the horse, the other is the rider. Then in a free-for-all the riders try to dethrone each other, and the one who is able to remain on his horse successfully through it all is the winner.

172. Hound and Hare Race

Divide the group into two teams. One team consists of hares, the other of hounds. The hares have a goal to which they can return, if they wish, and of course the hounds will play sentry to try to keep them from returning. On the other hand, the hounds will attempt to catch as many of the hares as they can and put them into their den.

173. Crows and Cranes

Have two goal lines, each about fifty to seventy-five feet apart. Divide your contestants into equal teams, placing one team on one goal line, the other on the other. A leader stands near the center.

One team is called "Crows," the other "Cranes." At a given signal from the leader both teams start marching toward each other. The leader will then cry, "Cr-r-r-rows!" or he will cry "Cr-r-r-anes!"

If he cries, "Crows," then the cranes try to catch the crows. Everyone who is caught must go to the cranes' side. If he were to call, "Cranes," then the crows would try to catch the cranes, with the same misfortune befalling those who were captured.

To make the game more exciting the leader will occasionally give a false warning, using such words as "crackers," "crawfish," and the like.

174. Tug o' War

You need a good strong rope, at least a hundred feet long. Choose two teams and place one group at one end of the rope, the other at the opposite end. Each contestant gets a good grasp on the rope. Tie a white handkerchief at the very middle of the rope.

Each group pulls in its own direction as hard as possible, and tries to pull the other team completely over to its side. The object of the white handkerchief is to give an idea as to which team is gaining the decision.

74

To add a bit more incentive to this game, fill a box full of candy bars or some other prize and place this exactly in the center. As soon as one team is able to pull the other team beyond the box the box and its contents becomes their property.

175. Horseback Tug o' War

Here is one for the boys or men to play. Divide your contestants into two teams with an even number of contestants on each team. Then have each team pair up, one member of each pair serving as the horse, the other as the rider. Stretch a long, strong rope between the two teams, which the riders grasp. Then, with each rider remaining on his horse and not at any time touching the ground, the tug o' war proceeds.

The horses may operate from either of two positions. They can go on all fours or stand upright. Perhaps the fray will be a bit more exciting if the horses keep on all fours, so that their riders are required to keep their feet up off the ground.

176. Comedy Ball Game

Set up your bases in the same order as for a regular ball game, except that they will not be nearly as far apart. The size of your picnic space will have something to do with this as well as the fact that the game is played somewhat differently. The fielders all have either bushel baskets or sacks. No ball can be fielded until it first comes into the basket or into the sack. Batters must stand with their backs to the pitcher, and bat with a backward motion of the bat. Also, when a batter hits a ball, he must run backward.

177. Human Croquet

You will need a number of cardboard boxes or some other series of objects to serve as the croquet wires. If you have enough people you can get two to volunteer for each wire, sitting down about three feet apart. Then have about four players and four balls. The balls are picnickers and each one is blindfolded.

Suppose you are shooting for one particular arch. You judge that eight steps will take your ball to the arch. Turn your ball in the direction you think he should go so as to go directly through the arch. Then instruct him to take eight steps. Start him out, and he will take eight steps. It may be that you have misjudged the angle at which you have sent him, and he will miss the arch entirely. If so, then you have to plan accordingly on your next shot.

You can also hit other croquet balls, as in the regulation game, and get your two free shots for doing so.

Specify that there must be no coaching from the sidelines, and that the balls must remain perfectly silent so as not to identify their positions at any time. Then it is up to the players to shoot with real marksmanship, and also to be able to accurately plan the number of steps which each ball should take.

178. Picnic Tennis

Take along an old tennis net and a basketball or a volleyball to your next picnic. Mark out a court, the size depending upon the number of players you are going to use, and place an even number of contestants on each side. Probably there should be no more than ten on a side, less might be better.

The ball is batted back and forth across the net. However, it must bounce once on each side before being batted back. Also, no one may allow the ball to hit him. If the ball does hit someone, a point automatically scores for the other side.

This game should provide a lot of fun and laughter, as the contestants must remain on their knees at all times throughout the game!

179. Discus Throw

Use a paper plate as a discus and see who can throw it the farthest. This will require some skill since the plate will have a tendency to sail in all kinds of awkward directions.

To make it all the more difficult specify that side distance does not count. That is, someone may throw the discus farther than anyone else, yet actually cause it to go only ten feet beyond the point from which it is thrown, when you consider the actual forward space covered. If there is a strong wind make use of it, and let the contestants throw the discus into the wind.

180.   Throwing the Shot-Put

Ask for all the strong armed members of your masculine group to volunteer for competition in the shot-put. Some of your most stalwart chaps will step up, expecting to show off their muscular skills. However, instead of a twelve or sixteen pound shot-put, have a large paper bag blown up. Competitors are to follow all the rules of the shot-put, including the motion of the arm, but instead of throwing a heavy weight will throw this paper bag.

181.   Ski Race

Dig up all the old skis you can, and take them along for a summertime ski race. Each contestant must wear a pair of skis, which will prove no end of trouble to him as he endeavors to be the first across the finish line.

182.   Sack Race

Give each contestant a burlap sack, into which he puts both his feet. Holding the sides of the sack with his hands he is to run, jump or use any other method by which he can proceed. At the signal "Go," each contestant heads for the finish line. Falling down does not disqualify anyone. All he has to do is get up and proceed on his way.

183. Bag Tag

Each contestant has a paper bag blown up and tied to a string, and the string is tied to the contestant's waist so that the bag drags about six or eight feet behind him. There are two goals, and the contestants run first to one goal, then back to the other.

As long as a contestant is on a goal, he is safe. When he is running between goals, however, the one who is *It* tries to step on the paper bag. If he succeeds then that contestant must remain between the two goals and try to help step on other paper bags. This continues until one person is left and he, also, captured.

If anyone persists in remaining on the goal anyone who is *It* in the center can point to him and count to ten, and he must leave the goal before ten is reached, or else he is automatically captured.

184. Pop the Bag

Divide your contestants into two or more teams. Line up all the teams at the beginning line. Opposite from the beginning line, about fifty yards away, place as many empty paper sacks as there are members of each team. At the word "Go," the first member of each team runs and picks up a paper sack. He blows it up and pops it, then turns and runs back and touches the next person in line, who runs and does the same.

185. Scalps

Give each contestant a paper sack of the proper size to fit snugly on his head. Then turn the contestants loose in a given area, with instructions that each one is to see how many scalps he can collect from the other contestants. As soon as anyone loses his scalp he is automatically out of the fray. If someone has collected a number of scalps but loses his own, then he must not only step out of the race, but turn over his scalps to the one who succeeded in conquering him. Scalps may not be held on the head, but must be protected merely by fast footwork or dodging.

The one who is able to keep his scalp intact throughout the game, while collecting all the other scalps, becomes the victor

186. Paper Step Race

Give each contestant two magazines or newspaper sheets. He can only proceed along the race by stepping on the paper. He may throw one of them ahead as far as he wants to, so long as he does not step on any grass in between. It is quite a feat to balance by one foot on one paper while trying to judge how far to toss the other one ahead and still be able to leap to it, and then, without putting the foot down, reach back and pick up the one from which one has just leaped.

187. Filling Pop's Shoes

Here is one for the small fry, especially the boys. However, girls can enter, too. Instruct each contestant to go to his father and borrow his shoes. The children then take off their own shoes and put on the shoes of their parents. They must keep the shoes on all the way from the starting line to the finish line. Of course the shoes will come off a number of times, and the racers will have to stop to put them on.

188. Altitude Championship

Boys like to see who can throw the farthest distance into the air. Give them a chance to prove who has the strongest "wing" by conducting an altitude championship at your next picnic. All you need is a good stop watch, some one who knows how to competently operate the stop watch, and a baseball.

At the signal, "Go," each contestant throws the ball into the air as high as he can, and the operator of the stop watch begins timing. As soon as the ball hits the ground, the watch stops.

Since a good stop watch will clock tenths of seconds, you should not have any difficulty in determining the champion.

189. Backward Throw

Use a bean bag, a pillow or some other cumbersome object. Have each contestant see how far he can throw this object backward. That is, he stands with his back pointing in the direction in which the object is to be thrown, and, without turning around, throws the object back over his head or over one of his shoulders.

190. Fifty Foot Dash

Give each contestant a piece of string fifty feet in length. At the signal "Go," contestants begin winding up the string. The one through first wins.

191. Indian Trails Race

This is an obstacle race for individual contestants. Set out a course ahead of time, and also prepare a number of assignments which must be completed along the course. For example, each contestant must find a certain type of leaf. Each one is to find a forked stick. Each one should find a certain shaped or colored stone. You can prepare your own list to suit your locality. If possible include a stretch of swimming to be done. Otherwise the rules are the same as for any race of any distance.

192. Hang Up the Wash

Hang up a number of clotheslines, as many as you think you will need, and keep a few more handy in case you have more contestants than you plan on. Then ask for girls to volunteer.

Give each girl a clothespin bag to tie around her waist, a basket full of some kind of outer clothing to hang up (same amount and type of clothes in each girl's basket) and a pair of heavy mittens which she must wear during the contest.

At the signal "Go," each girl begins reaching for clothespins and hanging up clothes, two clothespins for each garment. The heavy gloves will cause all kinds of fumbling and add to the merriment of the contest. If possible use mittens instead of gloves, as this will make the clothes hanging all the more difficult.

193. Scavenger Hunt

Divide your group into two teams or more with perhaps six or eight on each team. You can have as many teams as you wish. Give each captain an identical list of objects which must be found by each team. Then send them on their way. The team which comes back with all of the objects first, or the one which gets the most during the time limit which you set, is the winner. Have the group try to get such objects as: an acorn, moss from a tree, a four leaf clover, a needle from a pine tree, a crooked rusty nail and the like.

194. Somersault Race

Here is one for the boys. Line them all up evenly, and at the signal "Go," they must move forward on their hands and feet. However, at six or eight points along the racing area stretch a white cord. When each contestant reaches a white cord he must turn a somersault before he can continue on. At the very finish line have another cord so that the first one to somersault across it is the winner.

195. Apron Relay

Divide your contestants into two teams or more, dividing each team into two groups, one at one end of the running area, the other at the opposite end.

Hand an apron, preferably the kind that goes over the neck and is tied behind the back, to the first contestant of each team. At the signal "Go," each contestant must put on his apron. Judges watch so that no one begins to run until the apron is on and tied.

The contestant then runs to the other member of his team across the running area. There he stops, takes off his apron, gives it to his teammate, who proceeds to put it on and then runs across to the next teammate.

196. Carpenter Race

Give each contestant a large board or log, a hammer and a dozen nails. At the signal "Go," each contestant begins pounding his nails into the timber. The first one through is the winner.

197. Pop Bottle Relay

Select two or more teams with an equal number of contestants in each team. Each team lines up at the starting line and at the signal "Go," the first member of the team runs to the opposite goal line. There he will pick up a pop bottle, take an opener which is provided, open the pop bottle and drink it. As soon as he has finished drinking the pop he may run back and touch the hand of the next member of his team, who runs to the goal line and does likewise.

If you want to economize use lemonade or some other cheaper nectar instead of pop. Then, since you probably will not be able to have the drink placed in bottles, use cups and have the contestants sip the contents through straws.

198. Balance the Brooms

Bring along a half dozen or so ordinary brooms. Divide your contestants into groups of ten, as many teams as you decide. Each group divides equally, half staying at one goal line, and the other half going to the opposite goal. Give each group a broom.

The idea is for each contestant to balance the broom on one hand, and run with it as he balances it to the opposite goal where he gives it to a teammate, who then balances it as he runs back to give it to another teammate. This continues until each team member has covered the distance from goal to goal, balancing the broom.

Be sure to enforce the rule that carrying the broom will positively not be permitted. Also, if a broom falls to the ground, the contestant must pick it up at the point where it fell, balance it again and proceed on his way.

199. Thread the Needle

Your contestants must be in pairs, a man and a woman on each team. The men all stand at one goal line, the women at the other. Each man is given a piece of thread. Each woman holds a needle. At the signal "Go," the men run to the opposite goal, and try to thread the needle which the girls hold. As soon as the needle is threaded, the man takes it back to the beginning goal line, and the first one back is the winner.

200. Who's Got the Pebble?

All of your guests stand in a circle, hands outstretched in cup shape. *It* goes around the circle, carrying a small pebble. He pretends to drop the pebble into the hands of each contestant, and as he goes to each contestant, that contestant quickly folds up his hands. *It* drops the pebble into one of the hands, trying not to let anyone else see into which hand it is dropped. As soon as he has completed the circle, he cries, "Run!" The one who has the pebble then dashes for a goal, predetermined by the group. It may be a tree, large rock or the like.

The one who has the pebble must try to reach the goal safely, before anyone catches him. If he does reach it safely, then he is *It* for the next round. If he is caught, the one who catches him is *It*.

Games for Lawn Parties

201. Grey Wolf

This game is better played on a large lawn, although the area should not be too large, and it is much better to play it at night. If your group is very large you will need more than one grey wolf. For a small group one grey wolf is sufficient.

The sheep have a base where they are safe. So long as they remain there the grey wolf cannot bother them. Whenever the grey wolf catches a sheep he takes him to his den. A sheep can be released from the grey wolf's den if another sheep comes and touches his hand before the grey wolf can catch him. If another sheep comes and touches the hand of one of the captive sheep (but he can touch only one at a time) that sheep can return unmolested to the sheep's base.

Trademark of the game is the cry of the sheep, "Grey Wolf!" whenever the wolf appears near the flock. Of course the wolf will try to keep hidden so that he can pounce upon his prey. The sheep, on the other hand, will try to hide also and watch the maneuvering of the wolf without his seeing them.

202. Wild Game Hunt

Use a bean bag or some large but very soft ball, preferably of rubber construction. One of your guests volunteers to be the hunter. The rest of the guests will be animals.

Have the other guests count off by fours, more if you wish

to use more animals. The *ones* are lions, *twos* are tigers, *threes* are leopards, *fours* are panthers.

Then place half of your lions and tigers and leopards and panthers in one line, the remaining animals in another line, facing the first line about ten yards away.

The hunter can stand at either end of the line. He cannot stand in between the lines, however. He calls out any one of the classes of animals, who then try to change lines. As they do, he tries to hit one of them. If he succeeds in hitting one of them, that one becomes the hunter, and the hunter becomes an animal.

203. Streets and Boulevards

Have your guests stand in columns. Arrange them so that they will stand with their fingertips just touching when they hold their hands out. Then, when they turn in another direction, have them placed so that the fingers of each participant will reach to the elbow on the arm of the one to each side of him.

Select one of the participants as the leader, and have two others get into the group for a game of tag. The game begins by everyone standing with arms outstretched, touching fingers with the one next to him. Then the ones who are playing tag begin running up and down the boulevards formed by the outstretched arms, one chasing and the other pursuing. It is not permitted for anyone to break through the arms.

At a signal from the leader, who will exclaim, "Streets!" all of the participants drop their arms for a moment, and make a quarter turn to the right, and immediately join arms again, this time with different participants. They will change again in the same manner when the leader calls, "Boulevards!"

This will add no small amount of confusion to the one who is chasing and the one who is chased in this unique game of tag.

* * *

204. Fish in the Net

Have five or six volunteers stand in the middle between two lines. The rest of your contestants line up on one of these lines. All together or one at a time, however they choose, the contestants must try to run from the one line across to the other. In this sense, the game is similar to Pom Pom Pull Away.

In the center these five or six volunteers join hands, forming a fish net. As the others run through, they endeavor to capture one of them in the net. They must get him into the net and close the net before he can get out. When someone is caught, he becomes part of the net, and the game proceeds until the last fish is taken out of the lake.

205. Dragon's Tail

Have your guests join hands, all except one, who is It. The long line of guests holding hands make up the dragon, whose tail is its only vulnerable spot. The dragon rides back and forth, always remaining in one piece, and It attempts to touch the person who is at the very end of the dragon's tail. If It succeeds in doing this, then the one who is at the tail must become It, and It goes to the dragon's head.

By careful maneuvering the dragon will often be able to protect its tail for a considerable length of time.

206. Lame Fox

Someone is chosen to be It, the lame fox. The lame fox stands on a goal and all the other contestants come up toward the goal, taunting him. As soon as he decides to chase the contestants he may take three steps, as long as he wishes. However, as soon as he has taken the three steps, he must hop on one foot. If he catches anyone, then that one becomes the lame fox. This continues until everyone is caught.

207. Have You Seen My Dog?

Contestants stand in a circle. *It* goes around on the outside of the circle. Contestants stand with their faces toward the inside of the circle. *It* stops behind one of the contestants, and asks, "Have you seen my dog?" The contestant, who keeps his back to *It*, asks, "What did he look like?" "*It* then proceeds to describe somebody in the circle. As soon as the one who stands in the circle guesses the name of the person, *It* begins to run. The other contestant then chases *It* and tries to catch him before he goes around and takes his place.

208. Last Couple Out

Arrange your guests in couples, standing one couple behind the other in a line. Preferably have a boy and a girl, or a man and a woman, make up each couple. Then one man or boy stands at the front, with his back to the line behind him.

At the top of his voice, this one cries, "Last couple out!" The last couple then separates, the man going around one side of the line and forward, the woman around the other side of the line and forward. The point is that they are to try to meet again and join hands before the one who is *It* can catch either of them. If either of them is caught, then he or she becomes *It*, while the one who was *It* becomes one of the couples.

209. Three Deep

Divide your guests into couples, who stand in a circle. One stands in front of the other. One of your guests is *It*, and he chases another guest. This guest may dart in and out of the guests standing in the circle. If he is caught, then he becomes *It*, and must chase the one who caught him.

However, he can protect himself by standing in front of one of the couples. That couple then becomes three deep, and the one standing behind is obligated to run, or else get caught. He, too, can step in front of some couple, and the one standing in the back must then either run or slip to the front of a couple for protection.

210. Grab the Handkerchief

Divide your guests into two teams. Someone who is not a member of either team must be the leader. He holds the handkerchief. When the leader gives the signal, one member of each team, the members taking turns consecutively, comes into the center. While they stand there facing each other the leader will drop the handkerchief. One of the contestants must try to grasp the handkerchief and run back to his side without being caught. If he succeeds in doing this, the one who fails to catch him becomes a member of that team. If he is caught, however, he must go and become a member of the other team.

The game continues until all the contestants have been brought to the victorious side.

211. Strings

Extend a series of strings over all kinds of obstacles and around different angles. Give each contestant the end of one of these strings. Each contestant is to follow the string he holds, winding it up as he goes. He must go over, or under, or around each obstacle, following the route of the string.

To further complicate matters tie two strings together here and there. Make sure, though, that each contestant has the same area, or amount of area, to cover.

212. Human Ninepins

Let nine or a dozen guests stand together in a limited area. Each must stand on one leg, but may change from leg to leg, as long as he never stands on two legs at one time. Then, using a basketball or a beach ball, let the girl guests take turns rolling the ball into the group of men. The object is to try to cause one of them either to tumble over or to put two feet down at the same time. Each one who does is disqualified, and the girl who succeeds in bringing the disqualification about, is awarded a point.

213. Magnetic Search

Place a nail somewhere in the grass, at a place where you will be able to locate it if necessary. Then give each one of your contestants a magnet suspended from a string. The one who first picks up the nail will be awarded some sort of treasure as a prize.

214. Chivalry

Divide your guests into teams, the number of teams depending on the number of guests. Be sure to have an equal number of boys and girls in each team. In each team, divide the boys and girls into pairs, one boy and one girl in each pair.

The teams all assemble at the starting line. About twenty-five yards away place on the ground a collapsed folding chair for each team. At the signal "Go," the first couple of each team runs to its folding chair. The boy picks up the chair, opens it and seats the girl who then counts to ten as rapidly as she can. She then stands, and the boy folds the chair, puts it down and the two run back and touch the hands of the next couple, who repeat the procedure. The first team through is the winner.

215. Send a Telegram

Divide your guests into two or more teams, each team standing in line. Give the first member of each team an envelope with a telegraph message in it. Each envelope and message should be identical.

At the signal "Go," the first contestants tear open the envelopes and read the messages. They must then crumple them up immediately and throw them on the ground. As they do, they turn and whisper the messages into the ears of the next persons, behind them. Those persons turn and whisper the messages into the ears of the next persons behind them. This continues until the messages have gone through the line to the last two persons. They then run to the judge and give the messages to him.

Award first prize to the team which delivers the most accurate message, even if that team comes in last as far as speed is concerned. To further complicate things make the message a bit difficult to give from mouth to mouth, although do not make it more than a dozen words, if possible.

A typical message might be: "Aunt Effie's erysipelas has shown improvement after treatment."

216. Pillow Slip Race

This will be particularly amusing if you limit it to the men in attendance at your party. Have two or more teams, each with an equal number of contestants. Line up the teams at the starting point. At the signal "Go," the first contestant in each team runs to the opposite goal. There, on a chair or a table, is a pillow and a pillow slip. He must pick up the pillow, put the pillow slip on it, take the pillow slip off and place both of the objects back on the table, and then run back and touch the hand of the next one in line, who goes and duplicates the act.

217. Balloon Bust

Give each guest a balloon and instruct him to blow it up and then tie it to his ankle. Then each participant tries to break the balloons of the other contestants by stepping on them, the last one left with a balloon being the winner.

218. Daffy Relay

Divide your contestants up into two or more teams. Have each team count off. Then instruct the contestants that each of them will have to do his racing by a different strategy. Number one, for example, will hop to the goal line and back on one foot. Number two will go on his hands and knees. Number three will skip, and so forth.

219. Candle Relay

Divide your guests into two or more teams. Half of each team stands on one goal line, the other half on the other. At each goal line is a candle which is kept stationary, to be used in lighting candles which go out. At the signal "Go," the first contestant in each team lights his candle and then hurries across the racing area to his waiting teammate on the other side. If the candle goes out while he is running he must return and light it again. If he succeeds in getting across, keeping the candle lighted, he hands it to his teammate who endeavors to hurry across, without letting the candle go out, to the next teammate at the other goal.

This continues until each contestant has crossed the racing area, and one team is the victor.

220. What's Your Cargo?

Seat your guests in a circle. Use a bean bag or some similar object which you can throw and have someone stand in the center who knows the secret. He tosses the bean bag to someone in the circle, and as it is caught, he says, "Ships are sailing. What's your cargo?"

The person who catches the article must answer with something which begins with the first initial of either his first or his last name. For example, suppose the person's name is John. The one in the center could say, "Ships are sailing. What's your cargo?" John would answer, "Jewels." Or, if his last name were Smith he could answer, "Salt."

Whoever is able to answer a correct item may sit down. The others must remain standing until each one in turn catches on to the idea.

221. Wireless Telegraphy

This game should be played at night. Divide your guests into teams of five or more. Provide each team with a copy of the Morse code and a supply of pencils and paper. Then have someone stand off at a distance, and using a flashlight, slowly and distinctly give a message in the Morse code.

So word the message that the teams will not know what the instruction is until the last word has been deciphered. For example, the message might be, "Run immediately to the veranda." As soon as a team has deciphered the message, its members are to follow it out, and the first one to do so is the winner.

Suggest to each team that someone be appointed to read the dots and dashes as they are flashed, someone else to carefully jot them down so that they will not be forgotten, while the others look up the meanings on the Morse code sheet. Also, assure the guests that there will be an ample space given between each word flashed.

222. In and Out the Window

Have the guests stand in a circle and join hands. Then someone volunteers to be *It*, and someone else volunteers to be chased. As *It* chases his victim, they must run around the circle, going in and out under the clasped hands of those in the circle, which are held high. They run inside the circle under the clasped hands of two people, then back outside the circle under the clasped hands of the next couple, until *It* catches his victim. Then *It* selects the next victim and takes his place in the circle. The one just caught is now *It*. This continues until all playing, have been victims.

223. Treasure Hunt

Ahead of time hide clues telling the guests where they are to go. When they arrive divide them into groups of five or six each, and hand them the first clue, which tells them where the second clue is, the second clue telling them where the third is, and so on. Have approximately eight clues, planned so the hunt lasts an hour or two. At the end of the hunt have a buried treasure, which might be a box of candy. The hunters can either go on foot or in cars. If you wish you may have the hunt end at a place where refreshments will be served, or it can circle back to the starting point. You might give each group a telephone number they can call for instructions, in case they should get lost along the way.

*   *   *

Outdoor Stunts

224. Pillow Fight Championship

Bring out two pillows and ask for two men or boys to volunteer to battle it out with each other. After the two contenders have volunteered, fasten a rope to the leg of each one. Inform them that this is so they will not wander too far astray, and get lost from contact with each other.

Fasten the opposite end of each rope to some secure object outside the ring. Then have the contestants shake hands, after which they are blindfolded in the center of the ring. They then return to their corners.

While they are blindfolded in the corners, and unknown to them, the rope is shortened for each contender, so that when the two return to the ring, neither is able to reach the other.

However, and here is where the laugh comes in, the referee is supplied with a third pillow, unknown to the contenders. He moves in and out among them gently slapping first one and then the other, making each one feel that he is being hit but is unable to get a blow back at his opponent.

225. Barber Shop

Each team consists of two volunteers. Each contestant has a chair. One of them is the barber, the other the customer. Give each barber a shaving mug, soap and brush. Also give each one a razor, made out of wood, so as not to be dangerous. If you can get rubber knives at the dime store, those would suffice. Whether you use wood or rubber, put a little bit of vaseline on the shaving edge, to further complicate matters.

At the signal "Go," each barber must tie the apron around the neck of his customer and begin putting on soap. The judge watches each team to make sure that the face of each customer is thoroughly lathered. Then the barber shaves off the lather. The final judging, if the decision is close, will depend on which one has produced the neatest shave, that is, who has not allowed lather to drop down on either the customer or the ground.

The point is to see which barber can most neatly and swiftly complete his job.

226. Shoes in a Muddle

Have each of your guests remove his shoes. These are then placed in a pile some distance away from the spot where your guests line up. At the signal "Go," the contestants all dash for the pile at once. The fun is to see who can first find his shoes, get them on, and return to the starting point.

227. Gathering of the Nuts

If you are in a wooded section announce that you are going to stage a play. Solicit volunteers to act as props as well as characters. The more you build up your plans, the bigger will be the letdown.

When all are assembled, announce, "The name of this play is *The Gathering of the Nuts.*"

228. Firefall

Any area which has rocky cliffs can sponsor a firefall. Make sure to have official permission from property owners and conservation officials.

One group goes up onto the cliff and builds a bonfire as

soon as darkness has fallen completely. In the valley, and some distance away, the other group builds another fire.

As the fires glow the two groups sing appropriate hymns and choruses back and forth to each other. This continues until the fire on the cliff has produced a great many red embers.

Then someone below shouts, "Let the fire fall!" Using long poles, and working at top speed, the group above the cliff pushes the bonfire over the precipice, causing fire and sparks to fall cascading below in a thrilling spectacle.

229. Fire from the Sky

A wire, stretched from a high point to an unlit stick pile, can be used as a trolley to carry a kerosene-soaked receptacle, set aflame, which ignites a bonfire.

230. Girl Champs

A ridiculous softball game can be played if the men challenge the women.

The men bat and throw left-handed to even the competition.

231. Outdoor Shadow Pictures

Add a new approach to the use of shadow pictures. Hang a few large sheets between two trees. Use automobile headlights to shine onto the sheets.

Then have a cast act out shadow pictures, which appear on the opposite side of the sheet, viewed by the audience.

232. Dry Dousing

If you have a wiener roast near a lake some night, give two men a tub and ask them to go down to the lake and fill it with water. Instead they fill it with *leaves* and carry it back as though it had become a cumbersome burden.

Suddenly they lift up the tub and throw its contents on the audience, which expects to be drenched!

233. Heap Wise Man

After nightfall have someone appear in Indian garb who claims to know all the answers. He asks for questions to be written on slips of paper. These he puts into his wampum bag, and then proceeds to remove them one at a time.

The gag is that he has another set of stupid questions, with prearranged answers, which he reads to the amusement of the audience.

*   *   *

Water-front Games

234. Canoe Tilting

Place two contestants in each canoe and match only two canoes at a time. One contestant paddles the canoe while the other holds a long pole, the end of which has been carefully wrapped in padded burlap. The contest is to see which one can push the other combatant out of his canoe.

235. Tub Balancing

Here is one for the small fry. Bring a number of old-fashioned type wash tubs along and see who can stay in the tub and remain balanced the longest. The average contestant will tip over and slide into the water almost immediately but one or two will very likely come along who will show real equilibrium and who will be able to remain above water for several minutes.

236. Water Bronc Riding

Get a large watertight steel drum. Put it alongside the dock, and help each aquatic cowboy safely onto the bronco. Then leave him to his own, as the drum is very gently pushed away from the dock. Keep a stop watch to see which contestant can stay balanced on the bronco longest.

237. Greased Watermelon

Throw a well greased watermelon out into the water, not more than waist deep, if you are dealing with children, and announce that the one who brings it into shore first can have it. As a consolation prize for the many losers, be prepared to give each one of them a nice big slice out of another melon which you have brought along.

238. Underwater Keepaway

One person is *It* and the rest of the swimmers endeavor to keep a small, buoyant rubber ball away from him. The only hitch is that the ball cannot be thrown above water, it must be passed from person to person *under* water. At any time *It* is near enough the ball above water to touch it, he may retrieve it without a struggle, and the one who last touched it, or the one who is responsible for not having it in his possession, must trade places with *It*.

239. Water Baseball

This can be best played on a beach where there is a natural, sandy slope. Lay out a diamond similar to a baseball diamond, except that the bases will, of course, be much closer together. The bases are designated by poles driven down into the lake bottom.

Use a large beach ball. Proceed to play according to regular baseball regulations. You might have the outfield in deeper water, putting the better swimmers out there, so that anyone who hits the ball far enough will stand a good chance of getting a home run.

240. Davy Jones Football

Using rope and floats to mark off the boundary lines, stage a football game in water which is about waist deep. Use a rubber football and play the game according to the rules of touch football. That is, do not have any first downs. Each team has four tries and if unable to score must turn the ball over to the other side.

You may permit tackling, blocking and all the rest, because the water will retard any violent action. Punting is also in order if anyone can perform a kicking feat.

To get the game underway let the offensive team take the ball one-fourth of the way in from the goal it is defending.

241. Aquatic Basketball

You will need a slowly sloping swimming beach for this game. If possible mark off the boundary lines with cord. At each end of the basketball court place an inner tube to serve as the basketball goal. Then, using either a rubberized basketball or some other suitable object, choose sides and get your game under way.

Play in water at least waist deep. Instead of dribbling, allow the contestants to push the ball with the fingertips, through the water. In this way interceptions can be made.

Mark off, preferably by cord, an area five or six feet from the actual goal. No one may go beyond this. In other words, there would be no set shots under the basket. The only time anyone can go beyond the cord is to retrieve the ball in case a shot has been made or missed.

Whenever one of the sides misses a shot at the goal the other side takes the ball out of bounds. Otherwise rules are pretty much the same as those for basketball played on the regular court.

Or, if you wish, have someone stand at each goal to throw back any missed shots for the contestants to scramble after.

242. Ice Keep Away

On a hot summer afternoon nothing will be quite so unique at a swimming party as a huge cake of ice. Choose up sides for a game of keepaway. Instead of using a beach ball, use the cake of ice. Your swimmers will have a great time as they try to keep the chilly, illusive object away from each other.

243. Melon Keep Away

Another different version of the ever popular game of Water Keep Away is to throw a large melon out to the swimmers. Have a committee of judges keep time to see which side keeps possession of the melon longer. Award the melon to that side.

244. Davy Jones Keep Away

Use a bright red brick as your playing object in this game. Then choose sides, equal numbers on each side. By drawing sticks or by some other means decide which team gets the brick first.

The idea is that no one can catch the brick. Instead, if one teammate is to pass the brick on to another, he does so by throwing it into the water near this other teammate, who then must dive down and recover it from the bottom. An opposing swimmer will, of course, try to retrieve the brick first

245. Water Tag

One person is It, and must try to tag one of the other swimmers. Let the dock be the safety zone so that no one will get too tired. The one who is It must tag his prey in the water. Also, no touching back, so that the one who has been It will have a chance to rest. Make sure that a competent lifeguard is on duty at all times, in case anyone gets tired.

246. Water Gun Tag

One of the players is It, the rest of them are to be chased. It has a water gun, which he keeps loaded at all times. He must squirt water on some other swimmer, who may, of course, dodge or duck under the water or use any other means to keep from being hit. As soon as someone is hit by a stream of water, he must take the gun and become It.

247. Waves A Rollin'

Give each contestant a stick, or some other object which floats lightly upon the water. Be sure that each contestant has an object uniform with that used by each of the others. At the signal each object is dropped into the water. The contestant endeavors to propel the object to the goal line without touching it. He may blow it, he may agitate the water causing waves to move it along—but he must not touch it.

248. Cheese and Crackers

This race requires calm water. Give each contestant a paper plate, on which you have wrapped in waxed paper an equal number of cheese and cracker sandwiches. Each contestant is to swim from a given point, pushing the paper plate in front of him, to a designated point where he can stop and rest. If it is a dock, have him crawl onto the dock. There he eats his cheese and crackers as swiftly as possible, with a judge watching to make sure every bit is eaten, and as soon as he has the last morsel swallowed sufficiently so that he can whistle, he may dive back into the water and swim to the point from which he came.

249. Candle Race

Here is one for your better swimmers. Give each contestant a lighted candle, which he is to hold out of the water while swimming from the starting line to the goal. If the candle goes out along the way, he is disqualified.

250. Submarine Race

Divide your contestants into teams, preferably six on each team. You will need a one hundred and fifty foot rope for each team, as well as a small pulley. The rope need be no larger than clothesline rope, and the pulley will be fastened under water to a dock post or some other solid object.

The idea of the race is to have four team members hang onto the far end of the rope, each at a different place near the end, and dive under the water and stay there as soon as the "Go" signal is given.

At the opposite end of the rope the two other team members will pull the human submarines along the bottom of the water, to see which submarine can reach the dock first.

Of course, if any crew member on either submarine surfaces, his sub is automatically disqualified. Have someone at all times watching those who are submerged, to prevent possible accident.

251. Underwater Relay

This game is preferably played in water about waist deep. It can be played in deep water, but only by experienced swimmers. This operates on the shuttle relay idea, with half of each team standing at one goal and the other half at the other. The idea is for each contestant to swim under water until he touches the feet of his teammate at the opposite goal. That teammate then dives under water and swims back to the other goal and touches the feet of the one waiting there. This continues until the last member of a team has covered the underwater distance. Have someone watching to prevent accident.

252. Fifty Yard Splash

Line up your contestants in the water, waist deep, for a fifty yard foot race. Running in the water will prove a real test of strength and endurance.

253. Snorkle Endurance Contest

Give each contestant a large straw which he is to place in his mouth so that he can breathe under water. The contestants, at the signal "Go," submerge. If needed, each may have an assistant who helps hold him under water. The point is that each contestant keeps the end of his straw up out of the water. He breathes through this straw, drawing air into his mouth and forcing it out through the straw.

The winner is that submarine which can remain submerged longest.

254. Bulls-eye Diving

Place a large inner tube in the water, beneath the diving board. Each contestant has three tries, to see if he can dive from the diving board through the inner tube.

Or, if your group is small, give each diver ten tries and keep score. Be sure that the inner tube valve is *not inside* the tube, or injury may result. You may purchase such a tube, made especially for beach use, or, if this is unobtainable, you can tape the valve to the side of the inner tube to keep it out of the way of the diver.

255. Wireless Telegraph

Sound travels swiftly and clearly under water. You have discovered this if you have ever tapped two rocks together under water. While the sound cannot be heard above water, it can be heard for several hundred feet by anyone whose head is submerged.

Using this principle place your volunteers at some distance away from the spot where the rocks are to be hit together. If possible, do not let your contestants know who is going to knock the rocks together, or where this person is. All you tell your contestants is that if the rocks strike only once, they are all to race to one object. If the rocks strike twice, they are to go to some other. You might give four or five alternatives, which adds to the confusion.

At the signal, "Submerge!" your contestants go under the water. When each one is under, so that the water is still, the signal is given, and the race is on.

256. Search for Sunken Treasure

Get a number of empty coffee cans on which the lids can be forced down tightly. Place a slip of paper in each can, writing on the slip of paper what treasure that can represents, such as a candy bar, ice cream cone, bottle of pop and the like. Have these cans placed in the water ahead of time and let your swimmers look for them. If the water is clear enough put a few cans out off the diving board for your experts to go after.

257. Torch Relay

When night falls and you have built your bonfire down along the water front, have a shuttle relay in which each contestant must carry a fagot from the fire. This will create a scenic spectacle, and will involve a certain amount of skill in that the contestants must pass the fagots to each other without dropping them.

The game operates the same as a regular shuttle relay, with two teams or more, each having the same number of contestants. Half of the contestants are on one goal, half are on the other. Each contestant has his turn running across the racing area with a torch. Caution the contestants to take care to prevent accidents. Children probably should not participate in this relay.

258. Rooster Fight

Draw a circle in the sand about four or six feet in diameter. Two contestants get into the circle, arms folded. Each one must try to shove the other one out of the circle, keeping his arms folded. The one who is first able to shove the other one out of the circle is the winner. If you want to make it all the more difficult, set up a game on the basis of the best two out of three.

259. Foot Baseball

Use a beach ball instead of a baseball and play the game the same as regulation baseball except that you do not have a pitcher. Instead, when each batter comes to the plate, the catcher lays the ball on the plate, and the batter kicks it. Otherwise the game proceeds the same as regular baseball.

260. Poison Den

Dig a small circle, about five feet in diameter, in the sand Place a beach ball in the center. Then have all your contestants hold hands around the circle, and begin moving in a circular direction. The circle moves in and out toward the poison den, with the idea that each player is to try to force one of the other players into the poison den. Whenever anyone is forced in he must pick up the beach ball and try to throw it at one of the fleeing players dashing for a goal. If he hits one of them the one who is hit is out of the game. If he fails to hit anyone then he is out of the game.

This continues until only one contestant remains.

261. Buried Treasure

Divide your group into two teams. Designate an area for each team to operate in, each completely out of sight from the other. Then send the teams on their way, giving each a treasure chest to bury or conceal within the given area. No burying deeper than under six inches of soil!

After each team has had an opportunity to bury its treasure, have them exchange locales and see which team can find the other's buried treasure first.

262. Pirates' Gold

Prior to your water front party bury a treasure chest of some sort. Place candy in it, enough to treat the winning team.

Divide your guests into two or more teams, give each a clever treasure map, and send them on their way hunting for the buried treasure.

263. Water Volleyball

Divide your group into two sides of equal numbers and have them stand in waist deep water facing each other about 3 feet apart. If there are more than six on a side, make rows of six each for each side. Have someone serve a beach ball, the same as he would a volleyball, to the opposite side. Instead of a net, the ball must pass the three foot space. The other side then bats it back. As soon as one side lets the ball touch the water the other side gets a point and serves. Change servers with each point. A team may hit the ball only three times before hitting it across the three foot space to the group opposite. The first team to get fifteen points wins.

*   *   *

The Latest Games

264. Travel in Color

Here is a game to help make your trip more enjoyable. An old favorite with many, in the past, is to count "makes" of automobiles, to see which one has the most during your travels. One person would count all the Chevrolets, another the Fords, still another the Plymouths, etc., etc. The one having the largest number, at the end of the trip, or at a designated time, would be the winner.

You may also use a New Game with some real "color" in it. Make a list of the most popular colors of recent automobiles. If you are not familiar with them, telephone your local auto dealer and ask him what the most popular colors are in the new automobiles. If you have four on your trip, select the best four colors; let's say they are, white, black, red and green. These colors change, so it would be wise to make sure you have the popular four colors at the time of your trip. Name off the four colors you have selected and place them on slips of paper for each passenger to select, out of a hat. Make up a score sheet and keep track of each car you pass, see parked, or which comes into view, during the trip, awarding one point for the color seen. This contest can run for fifteen minutes, thirty minutes, or from city to city, or for the entire trip. A prize may be given the one having the largest score at the completion.

Other variations of the game, could be, body styles of cars, such as: station wagons, two doors, four doors, convertibles, etc. Many other versions of this game could be used as you travel.

*   *   *

265. How Far Is It?

Give each one taking part, a piece of paper and a pencil. Have them write down the left side of the paper the names of the cities and countries listed below. After they have completed listing the ten cities and countries, ask them this question: "How far in air miles, is it from CHICAGO to each of the cities listed?" Allow ten or fifteen minutes, before you call time!

List of ten cities (From Chicago, Ill. to)	(Correct answers) Air miles from Chicago, Ill.
BERLIN, GERMANY	4,410 air miles from Chicago
CAIRO, EGYPT	6,130
HONOLULU, HAWAII	4,245
MEXICO CITY, MEXICO	1,685
NEW YORK CITY	713
PARIS, FRANCE	4,140
SYDNEY, AUSTRALIA	9,272
SAN FRANCISCO, CALIF.	1,858
BOMBAY, INDIA	8,056
TOKYO, JAPAN	6,300

When "time" is called, have contestants exchange papers, and read aloud the answers given. Some may come very close, and others way off, which is good for laughs. The one coming closest to correct could be the winner and a prize awarded.

266. Travel 'Scavenger Hunt'

Make a list of 25 items for each person on your trip, making each list different. List items you should see on a trip, in the area you are traveling. Items could include some of the following: Shetland pony, man on a tractor, flag flying, water tower, red silo, windmill, white horse, green barn, airplane, etc. As you travel, give each one a list, and as they spot one of their items, they draw a line through it, after calling the attention of the others, to agree that it counts. The idea of the game is to be the first one to complete the list of items. This is a good travel game and keeps everyone looking for objects, and my how the time flies. You could prepare a "treasure box" and load it with "goodies," and show it to the group as the game begins, with the promise that the winner will receive the box.

267. Singing I Go Along the Road!

Everyone likes to sing, and here is an opportunity for all to take a part in making the trip more enjoyable. Select one to be "it" . . . "it" will hum a song, to see if the others in the automobile can guess the name of the song. As soon as someone guesses correctly the name of the song being hummed, they are "it." It's fun to use difficult songs, but they should be ones that are actually published. A variation of this game could be, to have the one guessing it, sing a bar or two, and if he can't, the turn still remains with the original player.

268. What Do You Know About the Trip?

Not only an educational trip, but you will find the entire trip will be more enjoyable and the time will go much faster, if you . . .

In advance of your next trip, write to the Chamber of Commerce, Travel Bureau, etc., requesting important information concerning the cities and states, you plan to visit. From the accumulated information, make up a list of questions on various parts of the areas you will be visiting. As you travel, ask questions of those in the automobile, about these areas. It will be fun to hear some of the answers they will give. You will always have the correct answer on your paper, and this will be educational for all. Listed here are samples of questions which would be of interest to all and make your trip more enjoyable.

Guess the population of the State we are coming into.
How many lakes are in this State?
Who can give us the name of the state capital?
Name the governor of this State?
What is this State noted for?
What is the population of this city?
What is this city famous for?
When was this State admitted into the union?

269. Use Your Name for This Trip!

Have each one going on the trip, write the letters of their name down the side of a sheet of paper. Behind each letter you are to write in items, as you see them, that start with that letter. You may list an item only once. Reason: You will see thousands of trees, but may only use one if you have a "T" in your name. (Example: You may have an "M" and see a Mule.) At the end of a set time, or at the end of the trip, it will be fun to see who has the longest list. Those with unusual letters in their names will find it hard to spot objects starting with these letters. This game is fun to play, educational, and a good way to pass away the miles. A little gift could be given to the winner.

270. My Trip to the Moon!

This is a game for an indoor party. Set your guests in a circle and one will start the trip to the moon by saying: "I am going on a trip to the moon, and I am going to take with me a 'Space suit'! The next one must repeat the same, and add what they plan to take along. Continue this around the room, and see how many items can be added to the trip. These should be items usable in a space ship. Example: Space helmet, oxygen, water, packaged food, flashlight, etc. This becomes more difficult as the game progresses.

271. How Far Is That Water Tower?

So that each one in your automobile may have a part, the driver will be "it" in this game. He looks down the road and spots an object that everyone can see plainly. He will say, "Joe, how far is that water tower from us?" Joe must reply by guessing how far, in miles and tenths of miles, it is. Driver will check mileage on speedometer, and as soon as he passes the water tower, he calls off the mileage. This is fun for a laugh, if Joe is way off on his guess, and good for a hand if he comes close. The driver will then select another object, down the road, and call on someone else for the answer.

Examples of items to spot: Large buildings, mountains, church steeples, grain mills, large trees, radio and TV towers, etc.

272. How Is Your Adding Machine?

Here is a travel game to sharpen up your arithmetic. As you travel down the road, the driver calls: "How is your adding machine?" He points to a license plate of a parked car and asks, "What's the total?" The object is to see who can total the numbers on the license plate first. Example: If the license plate reads XY 45983, the total would be 29.

273. Spot the Object! Make the Noise!

This is a game with "sound effects." The one selected to be "it" is to start off the game, by spotting objects, which he can imitate by sound. If "it" spots a cow, he will use the sound "moo" — a bird "tweet-tweet" — a train, "whistle," etc. The first one to see the object by sight, will get a point. After ten imitations, someone else becomes "it." Continue until all have taken part, then see who has the largest number of points.

274. You Can't Have One Without the Other!

There are many things in this life that are identified with another. When you think of one you think also of the other. Listed are companion words, and you will call off these words, to see if contestants can give the partner word.

Word list:

Ski	Snow
Boat	Water
Bullet	Gun
Tire	Wheel
Soap	Water
Bank	Money
Needle	Thread
Car	Gasoline — Driver
Hospital	Doctor
Lock	Key

Many more words may be added to this list to make the game more interesting. Give points for those giving the partner word first.

275. I'm Part of an Automobile! (Indoor circle game)

This is a variation of the old favorite, "Pack Your Suitcase Game." With guests seated in a circle, someone starts off by saying, "I am a_____," and gives the name of some part of an automobile. The idea, is to see how long you can keep going around the circle, till you run out of parts. As long as one is able to name a new part, he may remain in the game. Keep going until only one is left in the circle. No part may be used twice. Listed are a few suggestions, to start you off: Tire, wheel, aerial, car radio, radiator, fender, muffler, tailpipe, spark plug, steering wheel, generator, bumper, windshield, heater and horn. It will be interesting to see who can stay in the game to the end. An accessory for an automobile makes a wonderful prize for the winner.

276. Who Is the TV Personality?

Select five or six guests from your party and give them a slip of paper with the name of a popular TV personality. Use people who are noted for certain things that "stand out" when they appear on the program. Instruct each one that they are to stand up and try to imitate this person. The idea is to give a prize to the one doing the best job of imitation. This will be judged by how quickly someone guesses their person. Use personalities like: Ed Sullivan, Red Skelton, Jimmy Durante, Martha Raye, Lucille Ball and others.

277. Orbit the Earth!

We hear so much about orbiting the earth and trips into space, this could be very timely for any party. This is a question and answer game, which is good for a number of trips around the earth. Arrange guests in a circle and announce in advance how many opportunities each one will have to answer a question. Give each person three, four or five questions during the contest, which will give them as many orbits around the earth as the question is worth if it is answered correctly. A scorekeeper will keep the points for each contestant. Make clear to contestant that points depend on the difficulty of questions asked. Let them choose, if they want a question good for one, two, five or seven orbits? Listed are a few questions to get you started.

Good for 10 orbits: A cyclone and tidal wave killed 12,000 people in May 1965 — In what country did this happen? (Barisdal-District, East Pakistan)

Good for 5 orbits: On April 15th of what year did the Titanic strike an iceberg and sink? (1912) For an additional 5 orbits: How many passengers perished with the Titanic? (1,502)

Good for 7 orbits: In 1965, Charles Conrad and L. Gordon Cooper, orbited the earth for 190 hours and 56 minutes in the Gemini 5 craft . . . How many times did they circle the earth? (120)

Good for 5 orbits: How high is the Statue of Liberty from the base to the torch? You must come within 10 feet. (151 feet and 1 inch)

Good for 5 orbits: In what year did the Hurricane "Betsy" do its damage? (1965)

Good for 5 orbits: A question from the Bible: How many bumblebees did Moses take in the ark with him? (None, Noah went in the Ark)

Good for 2 orbits: (True or False) Franklin D. Roosevelt was the 33rd President of the United States! (False — 32nd)

Good for 2 orbits: Who was the 16th President of the United States? (Abraham Lincoln)

Good for 2 orbits: What was Albert Schweitzer noted for? (Healing the sick in Africa) (Doctor) (Theologian) (A Nobel peace prize winner)

Good for 1 orbit: How many calories in one slice of white bread? (64)

Good for 1 orbit: How many calories in a 12 oz. chocolate milk shake? (520)

These are just a sample of the types of questions you might ask. One or two really "super-dooper" questions might be included for a 15 or 20 orbit, but make them tough!

278. How Much Does It Cost First Class to Fly to—?

It's always fun to hear others' opinions and this is a game that could really be good for a laugh. Call the local airline and obtain the cost of first class fare to a number of distant cities. Have some destinations close by and others, perhaps in foreign lands. As you call off the name of each city, give the guests an opportunity to guess how much the fare would be. This could be a pencil and paper game or an oral one. If it is too difficult, you might call off three or four figures and let the contestants choose the one they think correct. This is a good game to get the group warmed up and also proves educational. If prizes are awarded, they could go to the one coming closest to being correct.

279. Don't Overshoot the Airport!

This will take knowledge, skill and some deep thought to bring you into the airport as planned! In advance, set up a list of questions, and make each question good for a number of air miles, if answered correctly. Each contestant selects, in advance, what airport he is going to and will know how many air miles it is to this airport. He is to select questions which will add up to the exact number of miles to his airport. If contestant "overshoots" his airport, he crashes and falls out of the game.

SAMPLE: If one of the contestants says: "I'm going to Mexico City airport," and your starting point is Chicago, the air miles he must travel would be 1,685. Now he may select questions good for 500 miles, 100 miles, 50 miles, etc., so that when he has answered the questions he will come out with 1,650 miles. Any number may play, and let them select how many miles they would like to try for. (Note: Listed are a few cities and countries with actual air miles from Chicago.)

City and Country	Actual Air Miles	Miles to use
Berlin, Germany	4,410	4,400
Honolulu, Hawaii	4,245	4,250
Paris, France	4,140	4,150
London, England	3,960	3,950
Moscow, Russia	4,980	5,000
Rome, Italy	4,815	4,800
Santiago, Chile	5,311	5,300

Let each contestant select the city to which he wants to go, before you give him the air miles. Questions may be selected from reference books or an almanac. Make a list of questions according to points.

280. Balloon in the Sky!

This is a real party game! On little slips of paper, rolled up and placed in capsules, write a number of things . . . These could be "a partner for the evening" — "a poem" — "a stunt" or "a question or an answer to a question." Blow up enough balloons for the capsules and slip a capsule into each balloon. Tie the balloons either in a cluster or use them to decorate various parts of the room. When the party is in progress, have each one select a balloon, give him a pin to pick the balloon to get the capsule inside. Proceed to have the contestant follow the instruction on the paper.

281. I Am a Poet and Don't Know It!

With paper and pencil, have guests print the letters of their name down the side of the paper. Now announce that they are to write a poem, rhyme, story or something of interest behind each letter. For a sample, if a girl's name is Dorothy, here is what you might do:

D — Down by the riverside,
O — Oh, what fun we had
R — Rowed our boat upon the shore
O — O the gang was glad,
T — Tom and Jack and Mary too,
H — Have fun where'er they are,
Y — You should have been along with us, you'd really get a jar!

It would also be fun, if you have an honored guest, to use his or her name. The poems will be "corny," as is this one, but loads of fun and laughs when read aloud.

116

282. Give Me a Word Pertaining to — ?

Seat the group in a circle and appoint someone to be "it" to start the game off. "It" may select an assortment of topics, but he will start off by saying: "Give me a word pertaining to _____." Example of topics: space, history, Bible, famous characters, travel, geography and etc. "It" will point to someone in the circle, then count to ten. As "it" is counting, the one pointed to must quickly give a word pertaining to that subject. If he or she is able to do this, they can remain in their seat, but if unable they are then "it." This is a good icebreaker or mixing game.

283. I'm Thankful for!

How often do we really stop to thank the Lord for all the blessings we have? Here is a game that has a little "Thankful" atmosphere for your party. One will start off by saying: "I'm thankful for _____." The next one repeats what he said, and adds what he is thankful for, etc. around the group. This is a fine game to use just before the devotions at your party, if it is a young people's group.

284. Space Game!

Here is another pencil and paper game, that is up-to-date, using our great space programs. At the sign "go" the contestants will write down every word they can think of pertaining to the space program or space travel. You may include planets, stars, etc. When you call "time," a prize may be given to the one with the largest list. Listed are a few to start you off:

Astronaut   Space Capsule   Missile   Nose Cone
Count Down   Space Suit   Launching Pad   Rocket
Orbit   Flight Time   Thrust   Craft   Outer Space
Satellites

285. I'm the Earth!

Set a number of chairs in a circle, and place one chair in the center. The person in the center will represent the world. Each of the others are given the name of a satellite, astronaut, or some star or planet. The one who is selected to be "it," must remember the names assigned to each in the circle, and call them by their SPACE NAME. "It" will be given a list of questions and answers to use. As "it" asks each, in turn, a question, they must answer correctly, or drop out of space. This is a game to test space knowledge and full of fun and excitement.

286. Party Skit

At your next birthday party, send a couple of sleuths out in advance to unearth information about the honored guest — taking care, of course, to keep the honored guest from knowing. Then plan a short play entitled "Scenes From the Career of _____." This will also work nicely into parties celebrating other events and anniversaries of a personal nature. Work in a generous sprinkling of humor, but do not overlook the spiritual possibilities for church parties, whenever possible.

287. Shadow Picture Skit

Always a good item for a party fun is the use of shadow pictures. Have someone come out in front of the sheet garbed as "Father Time." He begins to reminisce, telling of the events which have transpired in the lives of the honored guest and his immediate relatives and friends. As Father Time speaks, silhouette action takes place behind the sheet with light behind the actors.

288. At Christmas Time

At Christmas, divide your guests into groups and inform them that each is to present a short pantomime centered about some story, scene or situation directly related to Christmas. There is a wide possibility here, ranging from the more serious vein to the grind of last-minute shopping and the like. Onlookers, of course, must try to identify each scene as it is presented. If you wish, you may assign various Christmas scenes to the different groups.

289. "Radio Script"

Call on your literary minds again, this time for a "radio script" concerning some outstanding event on the annual society calendar for your church or other organization. For example, some of the guests are assigned parts to read in the broadcast, while others are to provide "sound effects." You must have a producer who tells the announcer (via a signal, of course) when to read the lead-in announcement. Then your trumpet fanfare, produced by whistling, comes in. Here is a chance, too, for a commercial plugging the weekly meetings of the society. The laughs come not only from the reading of the script itself, but also along the way as, from time to time, the producer points to various ones for the sound effects they are supposed to produce — everything from the screeching of brakes to the lapping of the waves or the distant hoot of an owl after lights are out (if it were for a camp scene).

290. For a Church Missionary Program!

If your church has an alert missionary interest, divide your guests into groups and either assign them subjects or let them do their own choosing. At any rate, each group is to act out in pantomime a missionary scene supposedly taking place where the missionary they have in mind is now laboring. See who can guess what missionary you are presenting.

291. How Is Your Memory?

Test the memories of your guests. Assemble a number of articles related to the church and young people's society activity — such as a religious picture, a Testament, a tract, a hymn book, an offering plate, church bulletin, missionary prayer cards, cross, etc. Add as many items as you would like to, and place them on a table covered with a sheet. Throw the sheet back for approximately thirty seconds, then instruct your guests to see how many of these church affiliated items they can list on a sheet of paper.

292. How Is Your Musical Knowledge?

How is the music I.Q. of your society membership? Find out by playing a few hymns and asking your guests to supply the titles. Another time, have your pianist play several numbers asking your guests to tell the time in which each is played; to make this as fair as possible, first have the pianist play a few illustrative numbers and explain the time on these.

293. ??? Where Will the Party Be????

Here is something for Christmas or Hallowe'en. On your invitations, print a big "?" after the word "Place." If it is Christmas time, rent a sleigh which will pick up the gang at church, or at some other designated location. A wagon, truck or automobile caravan can be employed for other seasons of the year. When all are aboard, set out for your party's location. For a novel twist, have the party all set up in the basement of the church which is, of course, kept locked and darkened. Take the kids on a lengthy ride, bringing them back to the place of starting.

At Hallowe'en time, select an old abandoned house not too well known to your group, and proceed to it for your evening's activity. Have four or five of your committee there in advance, ready to give forth with suitable howls, groans and the mysterious appearance of blue lights. This technique could be used no matter where you hold your party, for that matter. In case there is nothing spectacular waiting at the end of the ride, though, you had better provide some excitement along the way.

294. Refreshments for the Christmas Party!

For something different, at your next Christmas party, wrap all the food (except the beverages) in packages, and place them under the Christmas tree. Do not tell the guests what is in the packages, and wait to pass them out when it is time for refreshments.

120

295. Western Union Delivers the Lunch!

For something novel at your next party, have the doorbell ring near the end of the party and have someone deliver a large box all wrapped up like a special gift of some type. Act surprised and keep your guests guessing what is in the box. The box is opened in the center of the living room floor, and is found to be full of delicacies.

296. Party for Missionary Time at Your Church!

You can easily and profitably center an entire party around missionary themes. Meet in some large residence. Then have your program committee decorate several rooms to represent different mission fields. One will designate a scene from China, another India, Africa and the like. Your ingenuity will decide on the effectiveness of each room. Possibly you could get missionaries from each of the fields portrayed to send short, descriptive letters which could be framed for mass perusal. These rooms could serve as backdrops for your party, as you scheme your games and other activities to a missionary application. You might have this immediately after your church missionary conference and keep the missionaries over for an extra day, or you might work out your devotional with some missionaries. Food of various countries could be served in the various rooms.

297. Who Is the 'Odd Ball'?

Here is a game we have used since I was a boy, but it's always a lot of fun. Send someone out of the room. He is "It." . . . When "It" is out of the room, the remainder of the group decides which of their group is to be the "odd ball." The point is, each one will be doing something in unison when "It" returns to the room, all but "odd ball," he will be doing something different. The thing which he is doing must be concealed, so that it will be difficult for "It" to find out who is the "odd ball." When "It" returns to the room he is told to find the "odd ball." Give him just 5 chances, and if he catches "odd ball" then he must leave the room and come back as "It."

Index for Games for All Occasions